Ludoliteracy
Defining,
Understanding,
and
Supporting
Games Education

by
José P. Zagal

http://etc.cmu.edu/etcpress/

Design & composition by John J. Dessler

To Granny, Mom, and Amparo.

ACKNOWLEDGEMENTS

I would like to thank my wife, Amparo Minaya, for embarking with me on this adventure. Her patience and understanding cannot be described in words.

I would also like to thank my parents, Tilly Roberts and José Zagal, for all their support of both myself as well as my family during our stay in Atlanta.

This research also owes a lot to the guidance of my advisor, Amy Bruckman. Without her support I would not have been able to take the little "detours" that led me to find out what I'm most passionate about.

I would also like to thank the members of my thesis committee, Mark Guzdial, Janet Kolodner, Jesper Juul, and Michael Mateas. Their comments, questions, and insight have inspired me and helped me grow personally and professionally.

Thanks also to the GVU graduate students, members of the LST community, and current and former members of the ELC Lab. Their support, feedback, ideas, and friendship have been invaluable.

I would also like to thank the staff of the College of Computing and GVU for their help with all those "little" details along the way. Finally, I would also like to thank all of the students and teachers who participated in my research studies. None of this would have happened without them.

TABLE OF CONTENTS

ACKNOWLEDGEMENTS —————————————————————— VII

PREFACE ————————————————————————————————— XI

CHAPTER 1: INTRODUCTION———————————————————— 1
    Motivating Questions 1
    Overview 7

CHAPTER 2: THE STATE OF THE ART IN GAME STUDIES ——————— 11
    Definitions of Play and Games 11
    Multi and Inter-Disciplinarity in the Study of Games 13
    State of the Field 18

CHAPTER 3: GAMES LITERACY AND LEARNING ————————————— 21
    Games Literacy 21
    Understanding Videogames 24
    Learning Theory and Supporting Games Literacy 34
    Communities of Practice 36
    Knowledge Building 38
    Moving Forward 39

CHAPTER 4: NOVICES' UNDERSTANDING OF GAMES ———————————— 41
    Methods and Data Analysis 41
    Findings 46
    Characterizing a Naïve Understanding of Videogames 57
    Discussion 57

CHAPTER 5: SUPPORTING UNDERSTANDING THROUGH BLOGGING ———— 61
    Blogging for Learning 61
    GameLog 63
    Study 64
    Student Impressions 65
    Log Entry Analysis 74
    Discussion 86

CHAPTER 6: UNDERSTANDING GAMES WHILE CONTRIBUTING
    TO GAME STUDIES ———————————————————— 89
    Authenticity for Learning and Participation as Learning 89
    Game Ontology Project 90
    Affordances for Authentic Learning and Legitimate Participation 93
    Study 96
    Results 100
    Discussion 108

CHAPTER 7: DISCUSSION AND CONCLUSIONS ———————————————— 111
    Answers to Questions 112
    Other Issues and Findings 120
    Conclusions 123
    Future Work 127

REFERENCES ————————————————————————————— 131

VITA ———————————————————————————————————— 147

LIST OF TABLES

Table 1: Examples of ways of situating games as cultural artifacts 28

Table 2: Sample influential game mechanics from paper and pencil RPGs 30

Table 3: Categories and criteria for participant selection 42

Table 4: Participant pseudonyms and class details 43

Table 5: GameLog excerpt (Legend of Zelda: The Wind Waker) 64

Table 6: GameLog entry styles .75

Table 7: Distribution of frequency of styles used by participants 76

Table 8: Example Ontology entry - "To Own". 92

Table 9: User submitted example lacking enough detail 106

Table 10: User submitted example with extraneous information 106

Table 11: Expert evaluation of student contributions 107

Table 12: Motivating Questions 111

PREFACE

On the surface, it seems like teaching about games should be easy. After all, students are highly motivated, enjoy engaging with course content, and have extensive personal experience with videogames. However, games education can be surprisingly complex. In this book I explore the question of what it means to understand games by looking at the challenges and problems faced by students who are taking games-related classes. My results suggest that learning about games can be challenging for multiple reasons. Some of the more relevant findings I will discuss include realizing that extensive prior videogame experience often interferes with students' abilities to reason critically and analytically about games, and that students have difficulties articulating their experiences and observations about games. In response to these challenges, I will explore how we can use online learning environments to support learning about games by (1) helping students get more from their experiences with games, and (2) helping students use what they know to establish deeper understanding.

I explore each of these strategies through the design and use of two online learning environments: GameLog and the Game Ontology Wiki. GameLog is an online blogging environment designed to help students reflect on their game playing experiences. GameLog differs from traditional blogging environments because each user maintains multiple parallel blogs, with each blog devoted to a single game. The Game Ontology wiki provides a context for students to contribute and participate legitimately and authentically in the Game Ontology Project. The Game Ontology Project is a games studies research project that is creating a framework for describing, analyzing and studying games, by defining a hierarchy of concepts abstracted from an analysis of many specific games. GameLog and the Game Ontology Wiki were used in three university level games-related classes by more than 250 students. Results show that students found that participating in these online learning environments was a positive learning experience. In addition to improving their relationships to videogames as a medium, it also helped students broaden and deepen their understanding of videogames. Students also felt it provided them with a vehicle for expression, communication, and collaboration. Students found that by reflecting on their experiences playing games they began to understand how game design elements helped shape that experience. Most importantly, they stepped back from their traditional role of "gamers" or "fans" and engaged in reasoning critically and analytically about the games they were studying. In the case of GameLog, I show how blogging, in particular blogging about experiences of gameplay, can be a useful activity for supporting learning and understanding about games. For the Game Ontology Wiki, I show how it is possible to design learning environments that are approachable to learners, allow them to contribute legitimately to external communities of practice, and support visibility and access to the practices of a broader community.

CHAPTER 1: INTRODUCTION

Videogames are increasingly becoming an important part of people's lives (Pratchett, 2005; Cragg et al., 2006; Byron, 2008). Among some groups, such as college students, videogame playing is virtually a commonplace (Jones, 2003). According to the Entertainment Software Association (ESA), 75% of heads of households in the US play videogames and the average game player (not buyer) is 30 years old (ESA, 2005). These statistics are strikingly similar in other countries such as Great Britain, where 59% of the population between 6-65 years of age are gamers (Pratchett, 2005). For many, computer games are already a phenomenon of greater cultural importance than, say movies or perhaps even sports (Aarseth, 2001). Videogames are undeniably affecting our culture, the way we socialize and communicate, and how we think about the world.

The size and importance of the videogame industry is in contrast with our understanding of the medium of videogames. As recently noted by the president of the Digital Games Research Association (DiGRA), the field of game studies is still in the process of establishing its identity (Mäyrä, 2005), and with it, a unified language and vocabulary needed for describing games (Costikyan, 1994; Kreimeier, 2002). Game studies is an emergent field that is wrestling with what its fundamental concepts, ideas and theoretical models should be.

The challenges faced by this new field coincide with an increased demand for knowledge, skills and training for people who have an interest in learning about and studying games. The last ten years have witnessed an explosion in the number of universities and colleges that are teaching "game courses" and offering game-related degrees. Colleges and universities are not only teaching classes in game analysis, design and development, but they are also wrestling with the issue of how best to do it, what are the challenges involved and what they should expect students to learn. For instance, the education special interest group of the International Game Developers Association (IGDA) has spent over eight years working on a conceptual guide for game-related educational programs (IGDA, 2008).

Motivating Questions

What does it mean to "understand" games? What does it mean to have a critical discussion about them? What does it mean to be literate, or even fluent, in games? These questions are the driving motivators of this book. As I will show, there isn't really a consensus of what it means to understand games. When we ask people involved in their design and production, or scholars from the nascent field of game studies, we learn that they are also working on ways to figure it out. They point out the need for a unified language and vocabulary for describing games (Costikyan, 1994; Kreimeier, 2002) as well as a need for creating spaces for contributing deep, critical knowledge about them (Mäyrä, 2005). The International Game Journalists Association has also responded to this need with a guide that proposes a consistent vocabulary for writing about games (Thomas, 2007). Others, through a movement called "new games journalism", are looking for alternative ways to explore game design, play, and culture (Gillen, 2004). There is need for a space where ideas about games can be created, proposed, built upon and linked to existing knowledge that has been developed. Thus, my motivation is to make sense of what it means to understand games.

Motivating Question

What does it mean to "understand" games and how can we support learners in developing that understanding?

This is a broad question with many implicit assumptions, and I will begin to explore it by fleshing out some of those assumptions. Before I do that, however, I will briefly touch upon what "understanding games" means in the context of learners who are developing this understanding. These are issues that I will discuss in greater depth in the following chapters. In particular, I will use my discussion of the essential issues, questions and approaches that have been taken to the study of games (Chapter 2) to provide a definition for what it means to understand games (Chapter 3). This definition will be phrased in terms of what a person who understands games should be able to do. For now, when I write about someone who understands games, assume they should generally be able to:

- analyze games in a meaningful way,
- know how, and why, games help create certain experiences and evoke certain emotions and feelings in its players,
- know how games are used, and can be used, as an expressive medium, and
- have an informed discussion on the merits (or lack thereof) of a particular work.

Throughout this book, I will be exploring what it means to understand games. At the end, I will return to my big question, *"What does it mean to "understand" games and how can we support learners in developing that understanding?"* and offer conclusions about understanding and learning about games.

Question No. 1

What are the challenges of learning about games?

Researchers have argued that certain qualities present in the medium of videogames provide valuable opportunities for learning (Gee, 2003; Shaffer, 2006). For example, Gee argues that videogames can, under the right circumstances, create an embodied empathy for complex systems, thus allowing for deeper understanding of simulations (Gee, 2005). Games can also be action-and-goal-directed preparations for, and simulations of, embodied experience. In this way, they allow for meaning about what is being experienced to be situated (Gee, 2005). Is it possible that the affordances games have for learning make learning about games relatively straightforward? This is an unexplored question. On the one hand, one might assume that learning about games isn't particularly challenging. However, games aren't necessarily easy to play, or easy to learn to play (Gee, 2003; Squire, 2005). Perhaps these challenges also apply to learning about games? Additionally, if we consider that, generally speaking, achieving deep understanding of a domain or subject matter is hard (Bransford et al., 2000), there is reason to assume that learning about games can be challenging, even for those who play them regularly. If we want gain insight into how to support learning about games, it is important to identify, understand and address those challenges. Thus, the answers to Q1 should provide two things:

1. The means to outline the initial understandings and misconceptions that learners may have about games.
2. Suggest ideas and possible avenues for addressing the challenges identified.

These two points suggest further ideas and questions to explore. I will rephrase the first point so that it becomes Question 2 (Q2), described below. Later, I will use the second point to construct and define Question 3 (Q3).

Question No. 2

How can we characterize a naïve understanding of games?

If we expect people to learn, it is necessary to engage their initial understandings and misconceptions (Donovan et al., 1999). An important issue for promoting understanding of games, then, is to know what are students' initial understandings and misconceptions about games. Learning this will allow us to focus on strategies and approaches that may prove productive for supporting a deeper understanding of games.

These strategies and approaches must also take into consideration the reality of how games are currently being taught, who the students currently learning about games are, and what prior experience they have with videogames. The possible role that students' prior experience can play in supporting a deeper understanding of games leads to my next question.

Question No. 3

How can novices leverage knowledge from their personal experiences with videogames to create abstract and deeper knowledge about the medium of videogames, and what may we generalize from this?

Prior experience plays an important and valuable role in learning (Lave and Wenger, 1991; Schank et al., 1999; Bransford et al., 2000) . This is particularly so when the learner has personally meaningful connections with what is to be learned as the learner will then engage more attentively (Papert, 1980). Thus, students' extensive personal histories with videogames can be an asset in learning about games. But, it is not straightforward to help learners leverage their experiences and personal gaming histories to achieve a deeper understanding of games. The literature suggests strategies for leveraging experiences such as encouraging reflection and providing new contexts where knowledge from experience can be applied (for a review, see Bransford et al., 2000). I therefore explore this question through the design and use of two online learning environments. The first, called GameLog, is a web-based tool for maintaining journals, or GameLogs, of game playing activity. The idea behind GameLog is exploring how we can promote productive reflection on experiences with games. Those learning about games are usually game players and learning from game playing ought to be a part of any games curriculum. I designed GameLog to support productive reflection by providing learners with opportunities to articulate and describe their experiences with games, compare their experiences with those of other people, and allow them to compare their own experiences across time, and across multiple videogames.

The second online learning environment is the Game Ontology Wiki. The Game Ontology is an organic and evolving hierarchical framework of concepts, relationships and design elements derived from observations and analyses of videogames (Zagal, Mateas et al. 2005). The idea behind the Game Ontology Project is to explore how we can support students in getting more out of the knowledge and experience of games they have already had. In other words, can their knowledge of games be turned into a resource that may benefit others as well as themselves? My purpose in getting learners involved in using this evolving resource is to help learners relate their personal experience with specific games to the more abstract concepts and terminology in the ontology. I also want to provide a legitimate means for contribution and peripheral participation in a larger community of practice. By allowing learners to legitimately contribute to this resource we may also support the emergent field of game studies.

In creating environments for supporting learning, it is important to implement two major design principles for supporting learning: design to promote epistemological connections and design to promote personal connections (Resnick et al., 1996).

Supporting personal connections means that the activities of these environments should connect to learner's interests, passions, and experiences. The idea is that when activities involve objects and actions that are familiar, learners can leverage their previous knowledge and connect new ideas to the pre-existing intuitions (Resnick et al., 1996). This notion suggests the importance of helping learners use their passion for games and their gameplaying practices as a valuable resource. In GameLog, I aim for students to begin to realize how they can get more about of their regular gameplay experiences by reflecting and writing about them. In the Game Ontology Wiki, I aim for students to begin to connect the knowledge they have of games they have already played to more abstract and deeper concepts and ideas about games.

Supporting epistemological connections means that activities should connect to important domains of knowledge and encourage new ways of thinking. In the case of GameLog, I hope that by promoting reflection on their gameplaying experiences, students will begin to think more deeply about their play and begin to approach it in new ways. Essentially, I hope that using GameLog will help them think about games as game designers or game scholars, rather than simply as players or fans. In the case of the Game Ontology Wiki, I hope that student participation will allow them to have insight and access to the processes and discussion surrounding the knowledge building activity that is part of the Game Ontology Project. Participation should promote connecting what they already know to knowledge in the emergent discipline of game studies.

The importance of personal and epistemological connections to learning from experience has been cited over and over in the literature on promoting learning. (e.g., in research on reflection in practice (Schon, 1987), cognitive apprenticeship (Collins et al., 1989), and learning by design (Kolodner et al., 2003)). Each proposes different devices for promoting such connections. The devices suggested by these approaches lead to the hypothesis that novices can begin to leverage knowledge from their personal experiences with videogames by:

- Articulating, describing, and reflecting on these experiences.
- Comparing their personal experiences with those of other people.
- Comparing their personal experiences across time and across multiple videogames.

- Connecting their knowledge and experiences with abstract concepts and ideas.
- Using their knowledge and experiences to contribute to the creation of new knowledge.

GameLog and the Game Ontology Wiki have been designed to provide scaffolding for helping users reflect on, and leverage their game playing experiences in order to establish links between their experiences and the abstract concepts, language and vocabulary of game studies in general. Essentially, GameLog has been designed to support students leveraging knowledge from their personal experiences with games by helping them to reflect on their gameplay experiences. The Game Ontology Wiki complements this approach by helping learners use their personal experiences and knowledge of videogames to make connections with abstract concepts and ideas while contributing meaningfully and legitimately to the academic study of games. This last point is important not only from the epistemological sense, but also from the perspective of literature on communities of practice and knowledge building that highlights the importance that authenticity can have in promoting learning (Lave and Wenger, 1991; Wenger, 1998; Shaffer and Resnick, 1999; Scardamalia and Bereiter, 2002).

The research literature on communities of practice highlights some of the mechanisms that can encourage novice participation that is conducive to learning and enculturation (Lave and Wenger, 1991). However, in the case of a medium such as a wiki, it is an open question how these mechanisms can be put into practice, and how the online medium may change the role that novices play in these kinds of communities. Additionally, literature on knowledge building (Scardamalia and Bereiter, 1991; Scardamalia and Bereiter, 1994), a collaborative effort of multiple members of a community who work at the cutting edge to reformulate and deepen their understanding, also foregrounds some of the questions surrounding the role that novices can have in these communities and what sort of contributions they might make (Scardamalia and Bereiter, 1994). All of these issues contextualize the need for my fourth question.

Question No. 4

What role can novices play in a professional knowledge-building community of practice?

Authentic participation, in the context of learning, has been described as important for promoting learning and deeper understanding (Shaffer and Resnick, 1999). In the context of a knowledge-building community such as the Game Ontology Wiki, what exactly constitutes authentic participation? From Lave and Wenger's characterization of the role of novices in professional communities of practice (1991), we get the notion that even when novices engage in menial activities of the community, if those activities are important and necessary to the community and to achieving its goals, the novices will feel productive and have a chance to learn from the activity going on around them. However, what's most important isn't necessarily the activity itself, but rather the access and visibility that performing that activity provides to the essential values and practices of the rest of the community. Additionally, as highlighted by Collins and colleagues (1989), there are particular challenges to promoting learning through such apprenticeship when the skills to be learned are cognitive and meta-cognitive as opposed to physical. Collins et al. (1989) note that, in addition to the importance of learning skills and knowledge in their social and functional context, it is necessary that certain processes, which are normally internal, be externalized so that they can be observed and modeled. Thus, the essential question I am looking to answer here is how we can bring novices into a professional knowledge-building community of practice in such a way that they can contribute meaningfully and authentically while learning about games in a deeper fashion.

Over the course of this book, I will answer my motivating question, *What does it mean to "understand" games and how can we support learners in developing that understanding?*, by addressing the four smaller questions I have outlined.

Overview

This book explores the learning issues surrounding the creation of new knowledge and understanding about games and how to support learning in what could be called a new form of literacy. In order to properly situate the context in which learning about games is taking place, I will briefly describe the history of the study of games in Chapter 2. Most of the early work involving the study of games deals with definitions of the concepts of play and game together with understanding the role they hold in society at large. This chapter also explores some of the definitions that have been proposed for "games". Finally, Chapter 2 concludes by examining the recent history of game studies. Essentially, as the videogame revolution took off in the early 1980's, so did academic interest in games. To date, videogame research can be broadly characterized as taking a social scientific approach (studying the effects of games on people), a humanities approach (studying the meaning and context of games and games as cultural artifacts), or an industry and engineering approach (creating new technologies used in games and understanding the design and development of games). The research thrusts and current debates within the field reflect the field's nascent state, where appropriate methods, approaches, and vocabulary are still being defined and discussed. The state of the field of game studies serves as an interesting backdrop against which to explore how novices and learners can participate in learning about games while also contributing to game studies. These issues will be explored in further detail in Chapter 6.

Having explored the history of the study of games, I continue in Chapter 3 by defining what I mean by games literacy and focusing my attention on what understanding games means. In particular, as suggested by the research thrusts and interests of the game studies community described in Chapter 2, I outline the understanding of games as the ability to explain, discuss, describe, frame, situate, interpret, and/or position games (1) in the context of human culture (games as a cultural artifacts), (2) in the context of other games (comparing games to other games, genres), (3) in the context of the technological platform on which they are executed, (4) and by deconstructing them and understanding their components, how they interact, and how they facilitate certain experiences in players. When I discuss the role and use of GameLog and the Game Ontology Wiki in class (Chapters 5 and 6), I will refer back to each of these four contexts.

In Chapter 3, I also describe communities of practice and knowledge building as two perspectives on learning that I have used to both to guide the design of the online learning environments I designed as well as understanding their use (in Chapters 5 and 6). These educational perspectives highlight the ontological issue of understanding as situated in a socio-cultural context. As suggested by the literature in communities of practice, gauging the understanding of games would require situating the individual with respect to the beliefs, goals, and practices of a particular community. Understanding in this context is linked to membership and identity. Knowledge building, a process by which ideas that are valuable to a community are continually produced and improved, highlights the importance of focusing on discourse as a gauge of understanding and focusing on how discourse changes and evolves.

In Chapter 4, I explore the question of what it means to understand games by looking at the challenges and problems faced by students who are taking games-related classes. Essentially, this chapter explores my first two questions (Q1 and Q2). I explore these questions by reporting on the results of a qualitative research study in which I conducted in-depth interviews with twelve professors and instructors of game studies courses. My results indicate that learning about games can be challenging for multiple reasons. Some of the more relevant findings, in the context of the questions I explore, include realizing that extensive prior videogame experience often interferes with students' abilities to reason critically and analytically about games, and that students have difficulties articulating their experiences and observations about games. The following two chapters describe how students can be supported in learning about games by (1) helping students get more from their experiences with games, and (2) helping students use what they know to establish deeper understanding.

As described in detail in Chapter 4, many characteristics of the medium of videogames, including their non-linearity and duration (with games often requiring in excess of 20 hours of gameplay), conspire against their study. These issues of the medium highlight the importance of helping learners get the most from their experiences with games. Chapter 5 explores my third question (Q3) by introducing GameLog as an online blogging environment for supporting reflection on gameplaying experiences. GameLog differs from traditional blogging environments in that each user maintains multiple parallel blogs, with each blog devoted to a single game (Zagal and Bruckman, 2007). GameLog was used in two university level games-related classes, and students perceived writing GameLogs as a positive learning experience for three reasons. First, it improved their relationship with videogames as a medium. Second, it helped them broaden and deepen their understanding of videogames. Third, it provided a vehicle for expression, communication, and collaboration. Students found that by reflecting on their experiences playing games, they began to understand how game design elements helped shape that experience. Most importantly, they stepped back from their traditional role of "gamers" or "fans" and engaged in reasoning critically and analytically about the games they were studying. My analysis of the students' GameLog entries supports the students' perceptions. I identified six common styles of entry: overview, narrative, comparative analysis, plan/hypothesis, investigation, and insight/analysis. These styles align with practices necessary for supporting learning and understanding. Thus, I show how blogging, in particular blogging about games, can be a useful activity for supporting learning and understanding about games.

Chapter 5 explores Q3 by addressing the issue of how to help students get more out of the experiences they have with games. Chapter 6 explores the same question, but from another perspective: how to help students use what they know to establish deeper understanding. This chapter introduces the Game Ontology Project (GOP) and its use as a tool for helping students connect their experiential knowledge and observations with the abstract knowledge created by game studies researchers. Since students participate in the GOP by adding new content, it also raises the question of what role these students play (Q4). The GOP is a wiki-enabled hierarchy of elements of gameplay used by game studies researchers. As part of their regular coursework, students had to complete an assignment that involved the GOP. For this assignment, students had to find entries in the ontology and edit them by adding examples from games they knew well. My results show that students found the Ontology, and their experience using it, useful for learning. However, encouraging sustained participation was challenging because students tended to view the GOP as a static source rather than a participatory and editable resource. Finally, I describe how expert analysis of students' contributions to the ontology found them to be useful and significant.

In Chapter 7, I discuss the implications and conclusions of my findings in the context of the questions I originally set out to explore. I then summarize some of the lessons learned and comment on how these lessons might inform an agenda for further research. I conclude with some final remarks about the process of developing and evaluating socio-technical systems and comment on some unexpected results of the use of the environments I designed.

CHAPTER 2: THE STATE OF THE ART IN GAME STUDIES

This chapter will introduce and describe the nascent field of Game Studies. I will begin by outlining some of the different definitions ascribed to games, followed by a brief history of the academic study of games. I will provide an overview of some of the different approaches that have been taken with regards to the study of games and the different questions and problems that these approaches seek to address. Finally, I will characterize the "current" state of the field. This book deals with supporting learning about games and helping people leverage knowledge from personal experiences with games to better understand the medium. This chapter serves to situate it in the context of the field of game studies.

Definitions of Play and Games

"Consider for example the proceedings that we call "games". I mean board-games, card-games, ball-games, Olympic games, and so on. What is common to them all? -- Don't say: 'There must be something common, or they would not be called 'games' "-but look and see whether there is anything common to all. -- For if you look at them you will not see something that is common to all, but similarities, relationships, and a whole series of them at that." - **Aphorism §66, (Wittgenstein, 1963)**

Games have a long and continuing history in the development of almost every culture and society (Huizinga, 1954). However, as Wittgenstein noted, though everyone can agree on whether something is, or is not, a game, we cannot agree on a definition that encompasses everything that is commonly understood to be a game (Wittgenstein, 1963).

What is a game? This apparently innocuous question has been tackled by practically everyone who has studied games. Juul describes how "it is generally customary for writers on play and games to first describe their elusive character, discuss the impossibility of defining the terms, only to then use them freely and suggestively, indicating that there is after all some meaning attached to the words" (Juul, 2001). Part of the problem lies in the generally elusive and abstract qualities of the experience of play. The activity of playing games commonly brings forth a sense of make-believe (Caillois, 1961) and a sense that play is somehow situated outside of 'ordinary' life, even if it may absorb its participants utterly and intensely (Huizinga, 1954).

The definitions of games share much in common. For example, in games there is notion that there are goals and rules to regulate the achievement of those goals (Parlett, 1999). The game's participants make decisions and manage resources (Costikyan, 1994) while engaged in some sort of conflict or opposition (Avedon and Sutton-Smith, 1971). The outcome of the game is also quantified in some way (Salen and Zimmerman, 2004). Juul analyzed some of the most influential definitions of games and offered his own as a sort of extension and distillation of prior efforts.

> *"A game is a (1) rule-based formal system with a (2) variable and quantifiable outcome, where (3) different outcomes are assigned different values, (4) the player exerts effort in order to influence the outcome, (5) the player feels attached to the outcome, and (6) the consequences of the activity are optional and negotiable."* **(Juul, 2003)**

Juul's definition considers six features which, depending on the game, will be present in different ways. When features are absent something may be considered a game, not a game, or a borderline case. For example, Juul considers that games of pure chance are borderline cases because feature 4, player exerts effort in order to influence outcome, is not present. Watching Conway's game of life unfold or watching a fireplace qualifies as a watching a system with rules and variable outcome (1 and 2), but no values are assigned to the specific outcomes (3); the player is not attached to the outcome (5), and no player effort is required (6). Thus, these would not be considered games (Juul, 2003).

Juul's definition and accompanying analyses are interesting because he allows for a degree of flexibility with regards to what a game is. While he, in some sense, returns to Wittgenstein's original claim, there is a clear push towards exploring the borders between what games are and are not, as well as examining the relationship between them. While Juul's analysis is ambiguous when it comes to determining exactly what combination of features, or lack thereof, result in something being considered a game or not a game, it does provide a flexibility that allows for distinguishing different games from each other or anticipating new types of games that are just emerging.

As will be discussed later, definitions and the controversies surrounding them have been an important part of game studies. However, it is not the intention of this research to actively participate in that debate. Juul's definition will be used when necessary because it seems to be the one that provides the greatest flexibility for understanding what games are without being restricted to a certain medium or specific set of tools or objects. This is important because this thesis deals precisely with looking at how students make sense of games and their experiences with them. In a certain sense, I am implicitly dealing with definitions of games and what students understand them to be, while providing them with tools to support them as they position their understanding within the existing discourse of game studies.

Multi and Inter-Disciplinarity in the Study of Games

Prior to the late 20th century, the academic study of games was rare and limited to fields such as history and anthropology. For example, in the early 1900's, Stewart Culin wrote a comprehensive catalog of gaming implements and games from Native American tribes north of Mexico (Culin, 1907), while Johan Huizinga explored the importance of games and play as a basic human activity that helps define culture (Huizinga, 1954). As the videogame revolution took off in the early 1980's, so did academic interest in games. To date, the field of game studies can be characterized not only as multi-disciplinary but also as inter-disciplinary. Over the years, different fields and disciplines have demonstrated an interest in videogames and their study. The approaches taken thus far can be broadly characterized in three ways:

1. **Social Scientific Approach**
   - Studying the effects of games on people
     - What do games do to people?
       - Ex: Learning, Effects of violence in games
     - How do people create and negotiate a game?

2. **Humanities Approach**
   - Studying the meaning and context of games
     - What meanings are made through game use?
   - Studying games as artifacts in and of themselves
     - Ex: Affordances of the medium, critical analysis, rhetoric

3. **Industry and Engineering Approach**
   - Understanding the design and development of games
     - Ex: How to make better games
   - Games as drivers of technological innovations
     - Ex: Graphics, AI, networking, etc.

In addition to asking different kinds of questions, each approach tends to use different methods and tools to carry out their inv estigations. A large body of social scientists use quantitative tools and methods while a smaller group makes use of qualitative ones. Academics from the humanities tend to prefer tools and methods that are qualitative. The industry approach is practice-driven and usually less concerned with theory than the other two. Of course, these approaches are not mutually exclusive, and a significant part of game studies research blends them together. Interested readers can refer to Fullerton and Ito's work as examples of interdisciplinary work being done in game studies (Fullerton, 2005; Ito, 2005).

The newness of the field of game studies is also another reason for blurred boundaries between approaches. Williams, in a call for greater inter-disciplinary work in communications-oriented games scholarship, noted how the "study of videogames is poised to repeat the mistakes of past academic inquiry" (Williams, 2005). He argues that the newness of the field means that it is not bound to follow the traditional divisions of scholarly work, and that there is an opportunity to rediscover the strengths and contributions that different scholarly traditions can offer.

In the following subsections I present a brief overview of some of the research and work being done in game studies from each of the approaches.

Social Sciences and Game Studies

Broadly speaking, the social scientific approach has concerned itself with the question of "What do games do to people?" Using tools and methods such as surveys and controlled laboratory experiments, researchers have investigated both the positive and negative impact that playing games could have on people.

Among the possible negative effects of game play, perhaps the one most commonly raised by media and the general public, has to do with violence in games. What are the possible effects that playing videogames, in particular those that feature aggressive or violent elements, might have on children and youth? Social learning theory (e.g., Bandura, 1986) suggests that playing aggressive videogames would stimulate aggressive behavior in players, particularly because the player is an active participant (as opposed to a passive observer as in watching aggression in film and television). On the other hand, catharsis theory (e.g., Feshbach and Singer, 1971) implies that playing aggressive videogames would have the opposite effect by channeling latent aggression, resulting in a positive effect on players. Numerous reviews of existing literature have been written, and there isn't a clear picture of the effects of playing violent videogames might have (Griffiths, 1999; Sherry, 2001).

From the positive effects side, educators and learning scientists have also debated how to leverage the motivation students have for playin games and exploring the medium of videogames for educational and pedagogical purposes. Malone has explored the intrinsically motivating qualities that games have and how they might be useful in designing educational games (Malone, 1980; Malone, 1981), while Kafai has utilized the design of games by schoolchildren as a context for learning computer programming concepts and mathematics (Kafai, 1995; Kafai, 1996). Similarly, Squire has explored the use of commercial games as a means for engaging disenfranchised students in school (Squire, 2005). In addition to their motivational factors, Gee and Shaffer have argued that certain qualities present in the medium of videogames provide valuable opportunities for learning (Gee, 2003; Shaffer, 2006).

In her book *Life on the Screen,* Sherry Turkle explored how people who participated in online multiplayer games such as MUDs[1] used their experiences with the game to explore personal issues of identity (Turkle, 1995). In her book *Play Between Worlds*, T. L. Taylor recounts her experience playing the massively multiplayer online game *Everquest*. She sought to understand "the nuanced border relationship that exists between MMOG players and the (game) worlds they inhabit" (Taylor, 2006).

Finally, economists have also begun studying games, in particular massively multiplayer online games (MMOG), to better understand human behavior. The economic activity in these games is being studied as one would study the economy of a nation such as Russia or Bulgaria (Castronova, 2001). Different theories, such as coordination game theory, can be put to the test because games can produce contexts for natural experiments with a large number of participants and tightly controlled experimental conditions (Castronova, 2006). From this perspective, games provide a unique context in which human activity can be explored and better understood.

Humanities and Game Studies

In general terms, the humanities approach to game studies has concerned itself with the question of "What meanings are made through games?" Using tools and methods such as interviews, ethnographies and participant observation, researchers have investigated the various roles that videogames play in people's lives and activities and the meaning they assign to their experiences. For example, Consalvo explores how players choose to play the games they buy, especially how they negotiate how, when, and for what reasons to subvert a game's rules (Consalvo, 2007). It turns out that "cheating" is a very complex phenomenon whose meaning is continually negotiated by players, the game industry, and various gaming sub-cultures that revolve around specific games.

---

[1] MUD originally stands for multi-user dungeon. MUDS are in many ways the precursors of MMOGs.

Other researchers have focused on understanding videogames as cultural artifacts with embedded meaning, exploring what the medium of the videogame is, and situating it in context to other forms of human expression. Laurel's book *Computers as Theatre*, while principally focused on applying tenants of dramatic criticism to the design of human-computer interface design, describes how videogames are the natural result of computers "capacity to represent action in which the humans could participate" (Laurel, 1991). Rather than considering the computer as a highly efficient tool for calculating or computing, she proposed understanding the computer as a medium. The thesis of her book attempts to draw parallels between drama and the computer, with computers allowing their users to play equivalent roles to both the drama performer as well as the audience member. Throughout her book, Laurel uses different videogames as exemplars of many of the ideas and principles she tries to communicate. Jenkins (2003), on the other hand, explores the role that videogames play in a broader context he calls transmedia storytelling. In Jenkin's view, content moves between different media and videogames are a part of the general ecology of storytelling media that includes movies, novels, and comic books (Jenkins, 2003). Similarly, Janet Murray's *Hamlet on the Holodeck*, described the computer as a new medium for the practice of storytelling (Murray, 1997). By analyzing videogames along with other digital artifacts such as hypertext and interactive chat characters, Murray explores the new expressive possibilities allowed by computers. In particular, she views videogames as part of an expanded concept of storytelling she calls cyberdrama. Espen Aarseth, in his book *Cybertext*, disagrees with Murray's idea and holds that "to claim there is no difference between games and narratives is to ignore essential qualities of both categories" (Aarseth, 1997).

This disagreement has been called the "ludology vs. narratology" debates. The narratological view is that games should be understood as novel forms of narrative and can thus be studied using theories of narrative (Murray, 1997; Atkins, 2003). The ludological position is that games should be understood on their own terms. Ludologists have proposed that the study of games should concern the analysis of the abstract and formal systems they describe. For ludologists, the focus of game studies should be on the rules of a game, not on the representational elements which are only incidental (Aarseth, 2001; Eskelinen, 2001; Eskelinen, 2004). The idea that a videogame is "radically different to narratives as a cognitive and communicative structure" (Aarseth, 2001) has led the development of new approaches to criticism that are focused on videogames as well adapting, repurposing and proposing new ways of studying and theorizing about videogames.

Juul's *Half-Real* (2005) explores how videogames blend formal rules with the imaginative experiences provided by fictional worlds. He describes the tensions faced by game studies scholars when choosing to focus on the game or the player of the game. "We can examine the rules as they are found mechanically in the game program or in the manual of a board game, or we can examine the rules as something that players negotiate and learn. We can also treat the fictional world as a set of signs that the game presents, and we can treat the fictional world as something that the game cues the player into imagining and that players then imagine in their own ways (Juul, 2005)." Bogost's comparative approach to videogame criticism also stands out as one of the more recent steps in the direction of proposing new ways of studying and theorizing about games. In *Unit Operations* (2006), Bogost argues for explicating videogames through a new form of criticism that encompasses the programmatic and algorithmic underpinnings of games together with the cultural and ideological units.

Industry and Engineering Approach to Game Studies

The industry and engineering approach is perhaps the hardest of the three approaches to present. From an engineering perspective, videogames have been the context for a wide variety of technological innovations and advancements in areas such as computer graphics, artificial intelligence, and networking, among others. While the research pursued in these areas is mostly not about games, it is quite common for videogames to be used as a context in which to demonstrate the solutions and problems solved. A counter-example to the above is Mateas and Stern's interactive drama *Façade*, a novel videogame whose design and development resulted in contributions to the field of artificial intelligence (Mateas, 2002, Matcas and Stern, 2004).

From an industry perspective, a lot of game studies research can be seen as the academic response to the videogame industry's questions regarding the products it creates and sells. The main question this approach deals with can be summarized as "How do can we create better games?" with the accompanying "What makes a game good?" "Good" can be taken to mean many different things. Does the game provide an entertaining and engaging experience to the player? Is the game easy to learn and easy to play? Is the game innovative or does it provide the player with an opportunity to have novel experiences? Different approaches to studying this problem have looked at describing how to design games (Crawford, 1984; Rollings and Morris, 2000; Rouse III, 2001), extracting guidelines and rules of thumb for making better games (Fabricatore et al., 2002; Falstein, 2004), abstracting commonalities from games and understanding how they relate to each other (Björk and Holopainen, 2005; Zagal et al., 2005), and studying the gameplaying experience from the point of view of the player (Pagulayan et al., 2003; Sykes and Brown, 2003; Koster, 2004). Much of this research is also dedicated to defining and constructing a vocabulary for describing games and thinking through the design of new ones (Church, 1999; Kreimeier, 2002).

The industrial approach can be characterized as "design" or "product" driven. Methodologically, a wide variety of approaches have been taken. Most often, they are attempts to re-imagine existing practices in other fields and industries to the videogame industry. Pagulayan and colleagues, for example, have worked on developing tools and practices for evaluating usability in games (Pagulayan et al., 2003) while Bjork and Holopainen, borrowing from the literature on software patterns in software engineering have worked towards creating patterns for gameplay (Björk and Holopainen, 2005). Also, Bateman and Boon, using Myer-Briggs typology, have conducted research to create tools to help guide the design of games for certain demographic groups by incorporating elements specifically designed to meet their needs (2006).

State of the Field

Continuing with the growing interest in games, 2001 saw the appearance of the first academic peer-reviewed journal dedicated to computer-game studies. Espen Aarseth, the editor-in-chief of *Game Studies: The International Journal of Computer Game Research*, noted how "Computer Game Studies" can now be seen as a viable, international academic field (2001). Four years later, Frans Mäyrä, founding president of the Digital Games Research Association (DiGRA), posits that "there needs to be an academic discipline for the study of games" (Mäyrä, 2005). He argues that "games have their own distinctive features and fundamental character or ontology, which are not shared as such by other cultural forms" and that "having a discipline at the heart of a recognized academic field, with an identity of its own, is the best way of serving all those young students and researchers who are just waiting for an opportunity to specialize in games, to contribute to the deep, critical knowledge about them, and to push forward the logjam where the cultural status of games currently is located" (Mäyrä, 2005). Aarseth notes that one of the greatest challenges to the academic study of games comes from within the academic world because "games are not a kind of cinema, or literature, but colonizing attempts from both these fields have already happened" (Aarseth, 2001). He continues by describing the danger of ending "up with what media theorist Liv Hausken has termed *media blindness*: how a failure to see the specific media differences leads to a 'media-neutral' media theory that is anything but neutral. This is clearly a danger when looking at games as cinema or stories, but also when making general claims about games, as though they all belonged to the same media format and shared the same characteristics (Aarseth, 2001)."

Game studies, then, is in a state where researchers from multiple disciplines contribute to games research as a wider field. As such, it is currently developing as an extension and reformation of existing scholarly and scientific communities and practices. There is much discussion and reflection of the current state of the field and what the appropriate methods and approaches should be. Even the vocabulary and "basic" terminology is still being defined and discussed. Game studies, as a nascent community, is still experiencing "growing pains" as it begins to define its identity and essential problems.

In this sense, perhaps one of the greatest achievements the community has made lies in its success in "insisting on the legitimacy of computer games as objects of study in their own right, rather than as 'colonized' examples of film and narrative" (Murray, 2005). The formalist aspects of game studies have also helped call attention to the formal properties of games as well as "open up a range of productive questions about the definition of games, the form of games, [and] the boundaries between games and other cultural forms" (Murray, 2005).

CHAPTER 3: GAMES LITERACY AND LEARNING

In Chapter 2, I discussed the state of the art in the academic study and understanding of games. In particular, I illustrated how the game studies community is wrestling with what its fundamental concepts, ideas, and theoretical models should be. One of the consequences of the newness of the field is that there really isn't a consensus on what it means to understand games and what it means to be games literate. In this chapter I explore these questions. I will present a definition for games literacy together with a lens for exploring what it means to understand games. My definition for games literacy is grounded in Jim Gee's notion of literacy (2003), and the lens for understanding games is informed by the issues, questions, and problems explored by game studies, as seen in Chapter 2. I will use this lens for understanding games to contextualize some of the challenges of learning about games (Chapter 4) and the results of my work supporting learning about games (Chapters 5 and 6). Since literacy and learning are inextricably tied together, this chapter concludes with an overview of the theories and research on learning that inform my exploration of issues surrounding how to support understanding and learning about games. Thus, the goal of this chapter is to answer two questions: (1) what is games literacy and (2) how can what we know about learning inform our support of it?

Games Literacy

Early definitions of literacy focused on the ability to encode (write) and decode (read) written text at a level adequate for communication (Kirsch et al., 2002). The notion of literacy has been extended far beyond its original use in the medium of writing. As early as 1986, Spencer introduced the notion of "emergent literacies" in describing young children's media-related play (Spencer, 1986). Since then we have seen discussion around the notions of visual literacy (Moore and Dwyer, 1994), television literacy (Buckingham, 1993), computer literacy (Hoffman and Blake, 2003), procedural literacy (Perlis, 1962), information literacy (Bruce, 1997), and digital literacy among others (Gilster, 1997). One of the arguments given for an extended view of literacy is that communication in different media, such as television, film, and videogames, requires new forms of cultural and communicative competencies (Cope and Kalantzis, 2000).

As described by Buckingham and Burn, making the argument for the need to think about videogames in terms of literacy requires considering the possibilities and limitations of games literacy (2007). In particular, it is important to address some fundamental questions. For example, there is the implication that "games can be analyzed in terms of a kind of language – that they make meaning in ways that are similar, at least in some respects, to written language. It also implies that there is a competency in using that language that is gradually acquired" (Buckingham and Burn, 2007). However, the notion of game literacy also implies that the medium of games is distinct enough to warrant its own literacy. So, how do we define the characteristics of games as a cultural form? How do we differentiate them from other media? How do they create, or make possible, meaning and pleasure? Finally, how do players make sense of them and learn about them? As described in Chapter 2, many scholars have explored the characteristics of games as a cultural form and what differentiates games from other media. More recently, we have begun to see the kinds of meanings that games can create. In his book *Persuasive Games*, Bogost argues that games are a unique medium because they present a new form of persuasive rhetoric (2007).

Gee's *What Video Games Have to Teach us About Learning and Literacy* argues that literacy, as a way of understanding and producing meaning, needs to be situated in the context of a semiotic domain. Gee defines semiotic domains as any set of practices that recruits one or more modalities (e.g. oral or written language, images, equations, symbols, sounds, gestures, artifacts) to communicate distinctive types of meanings (Gee, 2003). If we take a sentence such as "The guard dribbled down the court.", and ask what it means to "read" it in the semiotic domain of basketball, at least two things are necessary: (1) the ability to decode the text, and (2) the ability to understand the specific meanings of each word in the sentence with respect to the semiotic domain of basketball. So, in the case of the above sentence, it is important to recognize the letters and words in addition to understand that "dribble" does not mean "drool", "court" does not have to do with legal proceedings, "guard" refers to a player in one of three standard basketball positions, "down the court" probably means that the player with the ball was moving towards his opponents side of the playing area, and so on. In addition to the need for understanding meanings in semiotic domains, literacy requires the ability to produce meanings, in particular to produce meanings that, while recognizable are seen as somehow novel or unpredictable (Gee, 2003). From Gee's perspective, literacy requires:

1. Ability to decode

2. Ability to understand meanings with respect to a semiotic domain

3. Ability to produce meanings with respect to a semiotic domain

So, by this definition, what does it mean to be games literate? Gee argues that videogames are essentially a family of semiotic domains (Gee, 2003).[2] For simplicity, we can consider videogames as a singular semiotic domain. The ability to decode is analogous to the ability to access the "content". For games, being able to decode is thus analogous to being able to play. Gee's second element, understanding meanings with respect to a semiotic domain, becomes understanding meanings with respect to games, and the third, produce meanings with respect to a semiotic domain, can be expressed as the ability to make games. Thus, games literacy can be defined as:

1. Having the ability to play games.
2. Having the ability to understand meanings with respect to games.
3. Having the ability to make games.

It is arguable that playing precludes understanding, which in turn precludes making. However each part of games literacy is related to, influences, and is influenced by the others. These interrelationships can be complicated, especially when we consider additional literacies. For instance, the ability to play a game can often encompass more than just knowledge of the rules, goals, and interface of a game. Playing a game can also include the ability to participate of the social and communicational practices of play. As Steinkuehler shows in her analysis of inter-player communication in the massively multiplayer online game Lineage, playing this game requires, among other things, knowing the specialized language used by the players' and the social practices they engage in[4] (Steinkuehler, 2006).

These issues notwithstanding, the focus of my work is on the second component of games literacy: **supporting the ability to understand meanings with respect to games.** For simplicity, when I refer to understanding games, it is implied that I mean understanding meanings with respect to games. Sometimes, such as when I discuss how the inability to play poses challenges to understanding games (Chapter 4), I will refer to the ability to play. Similarly, I will not focus on the ability to make games though, as others have suggested (Salen, 2007), supporting game design education might be a productive way of supporting games literacy. Issues of the ability to make games will, however, be discussed in the context of learners who are interested in game design, or are taking courses where the

---

[2]   Gee's argument for multiple semiotic domains is due the distinctiveness of different genres of videogames. This is something that will come up when I explore some of the issues that arise when we consider students as "videogame "experts in Chapter 4.
[3]   Ex: "afk gtg too ef ot regen no poms" = I'm not at my computer, I have to go to the Elven Forest to regenerate. I'm out of mana potions.
[4]   Ex: The player's are involved in a "pledge hunt", which requires certain coordination, commitment, and group expectations.

focus is on design (Chapters 4, 5, and 6).

What does it mean to understand meanings with respect to games? In the following sections, before describing the educational underpinnings that inform how I will support understanding videogames, I will provide a definition for understanding games. This definition is informed by the essential problems and questions of game studies as covered in Chapter 2, and also illustrates what it means to understand games in the semiotic domains sense that Gee refers to.

Understanding Videogames

In Chapter 2, I provided a broad overview of the current state of the art in the academic study of games. From this overview, and by looking at how the game studies community has explored, and is currently exploring games, it is possible to synthesize a definition of what the ability to understand games means. More specifically, I can look at the game studies work that has explored the meaning and context of games together with the work that has studied games as artifacts in and of themselves. Thus, I define the ability to understand games as the ability to explain, discuss, describe, frame, situate, interpret, and/or position games:

1. in the **context of human culture** (games as a cultural artifacts),
2. in the **context of other games** (comparing games to other games, genres),
3. in the **context of the technological platform** on which they are executed,
4. and by **deconstructing them and understanding their components,** how they interact, and how they facilitate certain experiences in players.

I will consider each of these parts of the definition a "context" for games understanding. Thus, understanding games in the context of human culture, is the first context of games understanding, the context of other games is the second, and so on. Each of these contexts synthesizes some of the essential questions and problems that have been part of the game studies literature. For example, the ludology vs. narratology debates I referred to in Chapter 2 were essentially concerned with exploring games in the context of human culture (first context of games understanding). What kind of culture are games? Are they narratives? If not, what place do games occupy in the ecology of cultural artifacts? This work, together with our understanding of affordances of the computer as a medium, have led to the exploration of the technologies on which videogames are implemented, and how these technologies afford certain kinds of interactions and experiences (third context of games understanding). Also, a lot of the work done in defining games has also dealt with the similarity, or lack of, that certain games may have with others (second context of games understanding). How are games related to each other? Finally, exploring the question "How do we create better games?" has led to game studies work that focused on deconstructing games and indentifying the components that make them work (fourth context of games understanding).

From a games literacy perspective, the ultimate goal is for students to be able to engage all of the contexts for understanding games I describe and possibly others as well. As I will show in Chapter 4, these fours contexts generally cover the spectrum of what is taught in most game studies courses.

First Context for Understanding Games:
Games as Cultural Artifacts

Understanding a game also means understanding its relationship, and the role it plays, within culture in general. A game is an artifact that occupies a place in a broader cultural context that includes other artifacts that aren't games. The meaning you can make from a game depends on understanding these relationships. Since cultural context can be quite broad, I will only discuss this issue from three complementary perspectives. The first perspective refers to the relationship that exists between games and other media. The second refers to relationships that can exist between games and certain media genres and/or artistic movements. Finally, a third perspective looks at how games can relate to certain cultures or sub-cultures in a broader sense.

Games often include references to and from other media such as print, film or television. Bolter and Grusin explain that "no medium today, and certainly no single media event, seems to do its cultural work in isolation from other media, any more than it works in isolation from other social and economic forces" (1999). For example, understanding a game such as *Peter Jackson's King Kong* would probably require explicating the relationship the game has with *King Kong*, the movie directed by Peter Jackson, and in turn, the relationship with the earlier movies also released under the same name. In another example, the single-player game *The Thing* promises, and indeed delivers, the opportunity to play with and within the most memorable elements of John Carpenter's 1982 science fiction film *The Thing* (Crogan, 2004). The game is conceived as beginning shortly after the point where Carpenter's film left off.

In some cases, the relationship between a game and an artifact from

25

another media may be primarily one of remediation, or representing one medium in another. For example, a game would remediate a movie if it allows the player to participate in the events depicted in the movie while maintaining the same narrative, characters and setting. Thus, understanding who the characters are and why certain events occur in the game is largely dependent on what is established in the movie. On the other hand, the relationship between game and movie could be complementary. Henry Jenkins describes transmedia storytelling as a "process where integral elements of a fiction get dispersed systematically across multiple delivery channels for the purpose of creating a unified and coordinated entertainment experience" (Jenkins, 2007). For instance, a game could offer a novel experience that enriches and extends on the fictional universe of King Kong by allowing players the opportunity to control Kong and learn about the giant ape's motivations and existence before the story in the movie takes place. While the experience of playing the game would be self-contained, it could not be fully understood without understanding its place in the broader ecosystem of media artifacts that together bring King Kong's fictional universe to life.

Games can also share aesthetic, thematic, compositional and structural elements from established artistic or expressive genres or movements. For instance, certain games have been described as sharing in many of the aesthetic and thematic qualities of noir film and literature (Davis, 2002). Understanding *Max Payne* as a game requires situating many of the decisions made in the design of the game with respect to the noir genre (both film and fiction), understanding what the conventions of the genre are, and also recognizing when adaptations or exceptions have been made. Davis' analysis of the game *Max Payne* describes how "*Max Payne's* noir elements are clear. But much of the reason they are clear is because the game makes a concerted effort to make them obvious. Its self-referentiality is understandable when looking at the rather overt nature of the features of noir narrative in general, particularly the visual elements. *Max Payne's* self-referentiality makes up for its contemporary setting, which admittedly hinders its noir-ness." (Davis, 2002) Similarly, understanding the game *Rez*, designed by Tetsuya Mizuguchi, requires knowing the artistic ideas of the Russian painter Kandinsky. In the end credits of the game, the game is dedicated to Kandinsky (Byron et al., 2006). *Rez* is a game whose carefully designed abstract visuals, highly layered musical soundscapes, and rhythmic pulsing feedback from the game controller all contribute to lulling the player into a mild trance that is evocative of Kandisky's ideas of synesthetic vision. In *Rez*, the perception of space and sound seem to become indistinguishable from each other as the player progresses, enabling the player to explore individual layers of tracks, add sound effects, and have it all blend effortlessly into a seamless whole (Kücklich, 2007).

Finally, games can also be understood as part of a broader culture or subculture where the aesthetics, language, music and other elements are those that are understood and valued by certain cultures or subcultures. For example, the *Tony Hawk Pro Skater* series of games are a relevant part of urban skater culture. The music in the games, the language used, the names of the characters, and even the locations available to the players can be significant to skater culture. The discursive practices of skater culture are reflected in the game, and making sense of the game requires an understanding of the broader discourse. There are other cases when these relationships are less evident and perhaps more complex. The historical simulation game *Civilization*, designed by Sid Meier, allows the player to nurture and guide a civilization from the Bronze Age until the Space Age (or more precisely, the year 2100). The game can be described as a historical simulation where the player chooses to control one of a series of authentic civilizations (i.e. Aztecs, Indians, Romans, etc.). However, the game assumes a Western (Eurocentric) perspective of history. For example, the game requires that "in order to pass from the Ancient to Middle Ages, you must develop monotheism, monarchy, and the alphabet- whether you're China or England" (Chen, 2003). Regardless of the civilization you control, the player is forced to follow a linear progression of developments similar to those of the nations of the Western world. Thus, understanding *Civilization* implies realizing the relationship between what the game models and represents as a particular understanding of history, in particular that of the Western world. Another subtle example can be seen in *Animal Crossing: Wild World*. This game is ostensibly a "animal village simulator" where the player controls a human character in a village inhabited by kind animals (Stang et al., 2006) and can be understood in the context of Western capitalist and materialist culture. An important part of the game's gameplay is purchasing and collecting furniture and other virtual items with which to decorate their home. The only explicit measure of the player's success in the game is determined by the quality (rarity) of the "stuff" owned, whether or not the player has completed collections of items, and how they are organized within the player's home. Players quickly find that their homes are not large enough to store all the items they own and are invited to take out loans to expand their homes. The tension between using money earned to pay off home debts or acquiring desired items resonates strongly with the issues of credit, consumerism and debt in modern capitalist society (Bogost, 2007).

Table 1: Examples of ways of situating games as cultural artifacts

Situation	Example
Game could be a part of a transmedia storytelling ecology	Some Star Wars videogames extend the universe and story beyond what is seen in the movies.
Game could remediate a cultural artifact from another medium	Some videogames are adaptations of comics, books, or movies.
Game could share in the thematic and aesthetic qualities of a broader media genre	Some videogames share the dystopian world-view and grim world outlook of a science fiction genre called cyberpunk.
Game could be part of a broader artistic movement	Surrealism, a cultural movement, uses games to provide inspiration as well playing games as a method of investigation.
Game could share discursive practices of a subculture	Some videogames are part of hip-hop culture.
Game could share values and viewpoint of certain cultures or societies	Many videogames set during World War II assume the perspective and values of the Allied nations.

Table 1 summarizes some of the different ways we can understand games as cultural artifacts. In summary, games exist in a broader cultural context, and it is important to use this cultural context in order to help understand a game and vice versa.

Second Context for Understanding Games:
Games in the Context of Other Games

Understanding a game also means understanding its relationship to, and the role it plays within, the landscape of other games. In addition to videogames, there is a wealth of games such as boardgames, card games, collectible card games, strategy games, wargames, role-playing games, sports, and so on. Many modern videogames are influenced or derive from non-videogames. Some obvious examples include remediated traditional board and card games like chess, poker, and solitaire. However, there are other videogames whose non-videogame legacy is less apparent. For example, the genre of videogames known as real-time strategy games (RTS) came from strategy games, which in turn owe much to strategy board games and their brethren wargames (Dunnigan, 1992; Crawford, 2003). Computer text adventures, including the original *Colossal Cave Adventure* (later renamed *Adventure*), computer role-playing games, and massively multiplayer online games (MMOGs) all share common ancestry with paper and pencil role-playing games (RPGs) that first appeared in the early 1970's.

Understanding the conventions and design decisions in many of these games requires making the connections to the original games, genres and creators. For instance, "experience points", "hit points", and "character classes" are all mechanics adopted from traditional paper and pencil role-playing games that are prevalent in many computer role-playing games today (see Table 2 for definitions of these). Explaining the design rationale behind the decision to use "hit points" often requires balancing the historical legacy owed to other games with the fact that particular mechanics used will be familiar to players. In other cases, the adoption of certain mechanics from one genre to another can be explained by looking at the role they play, and then adapting them to the needs of the other genre. For instance, the use of "character classes" was first introduced in the paper and pencil role-playing game *Dungeons and Dragons* (D&D). *D&D* is a collaborative game, and the use of character classes encourages collaboration by bestowing different abilities and responsibilities upon the players (Zagal et al., 2006). Modern team-based first-person shooter games such as *Team Fortress, Battlefield 1942* and *Wolfenstein: Enemy Territory* that rely on collaborative gameplay have arguably adopted character classes for similar reasons.

Table 2: Sample influential game mechanics from paper and pencil RPGs

Game Mechanic	Definition
Experience Points	Experience points (xp) are used as a meter of player progression in a game. They are usually awarded for accomplishing certain tasks. When enough xp are collected, the player controlled character is awarded with increased powers and statistics. The rewards for obtaining experience points are usually increasing and discrete. For example, the character might "level up" or get rewarded when obtaining 100xp, then 200xp, 400xp, and so on.
Hit Points	Hit points (hp) are a numerical indicator of how much health a character has. The idea is that attacks made upon the character will cause a certain amount of damage, which is then subtracted from the characters current hit points. The more hit points a character has, the more "powerful" he is due to the increased amount of damage he can withstand before dying or passing out
Character Class	Character classes are a game mechanic generally used for arbitrating the skills, abilities and aptitudes of different characters in a game. For example, a character who is a "Mage" might be able to cast magical spells while characters who are "Warriors" are not allowed to. Different games often define their own classes and usually a character cannot belong to more than one class at a time.

Another way of understanding games in relation to other games refers to the relationship between games that share a common pedigree, either in terms of their creators, shared characters, sequels and prequels, or all of the above. The relationships between sequels can be complicated. For example, the first-person shooter *Quake II* is officially the sequel to *Quake*. Both games were created by the same company, iD Software. However, despite the similar name, the sequel has nothing in common with the original game other than the basic gameplay and similar technology[5]. *Quake II* is set in an entirely different fictional setting and was named a sequel of *Quake* due to trademark issues and to leverage the popularity of the original (Connery, 1998). Other games, such as the real-time strategy game *Warcraft* and

---

[5]   The technology used in Quake II was based on that developed for Quake.

the massively-multiplayer online game World of Warcraft might share the same characters and setting, but vary significantly in gameplay. In the case of *Half-Life* and its expansions *Half-Life: Opposing Force* and *Half-Life: Blue Shift,* the creators decided to maintain the same gameplay and allow the player to experience the same story from three different perspectives. In *Half-Life*, the player controls a character who tries to escape from the Black Mesa Research Facility after a laboratory experiment goes awry and the center is invaded by monsters followed by military personnel intent on containing the incident. In *Opposing Force*, the player controls a soldier charged with, among other things, neutralizing Gordon Freeman, the protagonist of the original game. *Blue Shift* presents a third perspective of the Black Mesa disaster, this time through the eyes of a security guard. Both expansions share events and locations with the original *Half-Life*, and the player gains access to places that are "behind the scenes" in the original game while also catching fleeting glimpses and references of Gordon Freeman's exploits. Finally, to make things even more confusing, it is often the case that games released simultaneously, yet on different hardware platforms, might share the same name but be completely different in terms of gameplay. For example *Rayman Raving Rabbids* was released in mid-November of 2006 on Nintendo's Wii and Game Boy Advance (GBA) platforms under the same name. The characters and visual design, technical constraints permitting[6], are largely the same. However, the Wii version of the game was ostensibly a collection of short mini-games, while the GBA version is better described as a platforming adventure game with occasional mini-games (Navarro, 2007).

In summary, to understand a game, it is often important to understand its context with relation to other games as well as gaming conventions and mechanics that might be common across multiple games.

Third Context for Understanding Games:
Games in the Context of Technology

Understanding a game in the context of the technology and platform on which it is executed means situating the game in the context of the platform on which it is played and understanding the role that platform may have on the design and play of the game. Technological platforms both limit and afford the implementation of certain kinds of applications. The case of videogames is no different, and the restrictions imposed by limited memory, bandwidth, processor power, and storage capacity have, among other things, shaped and determined the kinds of games that are created. For example, the video hardware of the Atari 2600 only allowed for two sprites (two-dimensional images that are integrated or composited

---

[6] Nintendo's Game Boy Advance is a hand-held machine with a smaller screen and lower resolution and color depth than the Wii.

31

onto a larger scene), thus limiting the number of moving objects that could be shown on screen. Although programmers were able to squeeze extra performance through clever technical tricks, the end result is that the video hardware still severely limits what Atari 2600 games can look like. The resulting visual style of these games, in particular the "stripe-colored" sprites, is a trademark of Atari 2600 games (Bogost and Montfort, 2007). While hardware can limit, it can also offer new possibilities. For example, localization technology available in many mobile phones has enabled the design of location-based games that use information of the player's location in the real world to affect gameplay. BotFighters is an action game with a robot theme. In the game, players must locate and shoot at each other using their mobile phones. Mobile positioning is used to determine whether players are close enough to each other in the real world to be able to hit each other in BotFighters virtual world (Dodson, 2002). Novel interface hardware often broadens the design space of games by allowing for novel gameplay and interactions previously unimagined. The motion-sensing capabilities of the controllers for Nintendo's Wii game console are but a recent example of how hardware innovations can broaden the possibilities for new types of games.

In summary, videogames are implemented on technological platforms that shape the form and functionalities and experiences they can offer. It is often important to understand the technological platform and its relationship to a particular videogame in order to better understand it.

Fourth Context for Understanding Games:
The Structure and Components of Games

Understanding the structure of games is akin to being able to identify the different components that make up a game and how they interact with each other. If we go back to Gee's notion of literacy, this means understanding the design grammars of semiotic domains (Gee, 2003). In other words, recognizing and understanding the principles, patterns and procedures to the construction of games. What are the underlying models? What choices and actions does the player have available to him or her? What are the core elements of gameplay? What are the basic patterns of the game and how are they combined or recombined? For example, understanding most of the games in the *Legend of Zelda* series includes understanding the cyclical nature of the activities the player is required to accomplish. The player is usually required to (1) find the entrance to a dungeon, (2) enter the dungeon, (3) discover a treasure, find keys, a map, and a compass, (4) defeat a monster at the "bottom" of the dungeon, and (5) obtain an item or power necessary for the next challenge. Usually, the item or power obtained at the end of a dungeon will be required to locate or gain access to the location of the next dungeon. In the beginning of most *Legend of*

Zelda games, the player has no items and very few possibilities for action. Progress in the game depends on finding new items (the first item found is usually a sword that allows the player to fight enemies) and using them to gain access to new locations. As more items are obtained, the player must figure out how to use them in combinations that become increasingly more complex. By the end of the game, the player is usually quite adept at figuring out what item to use and when. As Gingold describes, "a key property of games is recombining familiar elements into novel configurations" (2003). In this sense, identifying what those elements are is an important aspect of understanding games structurally.

In addition to being able to able pick out elements of a game's design, it is important to understand how the interaction between these elements helps create a certain experience for the player. Understanding a game from this perspective is akin to being able to articulate why playing a game makes the player feel a certain way. From a game designer's perspective, this sort of insight and understanding is crucial when trying to map the design goals (I want the players to have this kind of experience) with a means of achieving those goals (I will use these elements, in these ways). Schell and Shochet describe how they designed *Pirates of the Caribbean: Battle for Buccaneer Gold* so as to provide an engaging five minute experience that was exciting to play, culminated in a climactic battle, and made players feel in control of their destiny (2001). *Pirates*, an interactive theme park ride based on the classic Pirates of the Caribbean attraction at Disneyland, allows four players to man a ship and attempt to defeat enemy pirate ships, forts, and monsters while collecting as much gold as possible. One player steers the ship, while the other three man six cannons used to defeat enemies. The designers used numerous elements, such as "special" enemy ships, sneak attacks, and architectural "weenies[7]" to guide the players towards the islands where "the coolest action takes place" (Schell and Shochet, 2001). Toru Iwatani, designer of *Pac-Man*, describes how the AI routines for each of the enemy ghosts that chase the player were designed so that the ghosts would get closer to Pac Man in a natural way and avoid discouraging the players by having them feel that they are constantly under attack (Mateas, 2003). Additionally, the ghosts alternate between chasing the player and dispersing, allowing the player some room to breathe, thus providing an experience of greater tension as the ghosts "attack" more frequently. In order to really understand Pac-Man, to understand the player experience and the player interpretations supported by the experience, requires a detailed understanding of the AI of the ghosts (Mateas, 2003).

In summary, to better understand a game it is important to understanding its components, how they interact, and how they facilitate certain experiences in players.

---

[7] "Weenies" are, as coined by Walt Disney, a technique originally used to guide stage dogs in movie sets. A classic architectural "weenie" is the castle at Disneyland which provides a reference point for park visitors as well as drawing the eye, and with it the visitor.

Learning Theory and Supporting Games Literacy

In the preceding sections I have described what I mean by games literacy, and more specifically, what I mean by understanding games. I argued that we can deconstruct the meaning of understanding games by analyzing them in four contexts: (1) games as cultural artifacts, (2) in the context of other games, (3) in the context of technology, and by (4) deconstructing them and understanding their components, how they interact, and how they facilitate certain experiences in players. However, I have not yet explored how learning theory will support the approach I take towards supporting understanding and learning about games. In the rest of this chapter, I will describe, using what we know about communities of practice and knowledge building, the educational perspectives that will inform how I will support understanding games among students who are learning about games.

Games for Learning

Umberto Eco argued that "if you want to use television to teach somebody, you must first teach them how to use television" (Eco, 1979). His argument about television can be applied equally to the domain of games and videogames. However, when people think of games and learning, what comes to mind most often is thinking about the use of games for learning and education. Educational research has a relatively long tradition of examining the use of games for education, in particular thanks to the prevalent view that play is a crucial method through which we test ideas, develop new skills, and participate in social roles (Piaget, 1962; Vygotsky, 1978). Recent technological advances, coupled with a better understanding of the medium of games, have led to a renewed interest and advocacy for the use and design of game-based learning enviroments (Gee, 2003; Shaffer, 2006; Dipietro et al., 2007; Barab et al., In press; Ketelhut et al., In Press). However, as I have explained earlier, this dissertation will not address the issues surrounding the use of games for learning.

One of the contributions of this dissertation comes from turning the question of How do we use games for learning around, and asking instead, what do people who play videogames know and learn about videogames? This is a research area that has largely gone unexplored and I argue that by looking at the difficulties involved in learning about games we can gain insight into the issues faced when using videogames for pedagogical purposes. Studying games and learning how to design them is a relatively new domain of study in higher education when compared to other domains such as mathematics, science, or literature. Studying students learning about games provides a unique context that is largely unseen in traditional educational research: learners usually have extensive personal backgrounds and experience with games, they are highly motivated to study and learn about them, and they have strong emotional and personal connections to games. From this perspective, many of the traditional "big problems" in learning research, such as lack of motivation and lack of connections to learners "real lives", are minimized. So, what insights might be gained with respect to learning in this particular context? For example, in what ways will their knowledge and skills from games transfer to higher education?

Contrary to educational research in other areas, such as science or writing, there isn't a clear idea of what it means to understand videogames in general, or even what it means to a understand a particular videogame. If we consider the issues of learning about something as specific as, say, the physics of light, the educational community has established what it means to understand, what typical issues a learner may be confused about, what naïve understanding looks like, and so on. For example, there is extensive research suggesting that middle-school students often interpret "light" as relating to light sources or lighting effects, rather than as a form of energy propagating through space (Guesne, 1985; Feher and Rice, 1988; Brickhouse, 1994; Shapiro, 1994). We know a lot about what a learner goes through when learning about the physics of light and can thus design and develop socio-technical systems to better support them and assess whether or not they have achieved the necessary level of understanding (Linn et al., 1998). This is not the case for learning about games. Also, save for a few exceptions (Holopainen et al., 2007; Salen, 2007), the question of how do we learn about games, what skills and knowledge should novice game designers and scholars develop, and what challenges do they face has also been largely unexplored by the game studies community. Bringing an educational point of view to the issues of studying games is another of the contributions of this dissertation.

Given these issues, what learning theories and pedagogies should we consider to better understand and support learning about games? Answering this question depends, to a large degree, on what exactly will be studied and what the unit of analysis for this will be. For my research, theories and pedagogies whose strength lie in explaining cognitive processes in an individual are not the most appropriate. The reason for this is that my focus is not on studying individual learners as they play a particular game or set of games, and then exploring what they may or may not have learned about games from that experience. Rather, I concern myself with the social and collaborative aspects of learning and how to support reflection and participation through the use of collaborative learning environments. My focus is also on studying people who are interested or curious about pursuing careers that somehow revolve around, or include games. These are people who might be interested in working in the games industry or engaging in games research. Many of these people see games as playing an important part in their lives and identify themselves with a broader community for whom games are important professionally. Finally, as was seen in Chapter 2, we are currently in a period where much knowledge is being created surrounding games, what they are, and what they could be. The current state of the field of game studies is but one example of this. From this perspective, the people I have studied will have to not only engage in learning about games, but also in defining and articulating new ideas and concepts.

In the case of my research on supporting learning about games, I have chosen to focus on theories and pedagogies of learning that focus on the social aspects of learning, and collaboration, particularly those that consider learning in the context of a broader community and its practices, and the processes through which learning, new knowledge, and understanding are created. The following sections will describe communities of practice and knowledge building as two perspectives on learning that I have used both to guide the design of the online learning environments I designed as well as to understand their use (see Chapter 5 and Chapter 6).

Communities of Practice

Lave and Wenger (1991) proposed the term "communities of practice" to highlight the importance of activity in linking individuals to communities, and of communities to legitimizing individual practices. A community of practice involves a collection of individuals sharing mutually-defined practices, beliefs, and understandings over an extended time frame in the pursuit of a shared enterprise (Wenger, 1998). Roth (1998) suggested that these kinds of communities "are identified by the common tasks members engage in and the associated practices and resources, unquestioned background assumptions, common sense, and mundane reason they share".

The literature on communities of practice holds that learning involves participation as a way of learning – of both absorbing and being absorbed in – a "culture of practice" (Lave and Wenger, 1991). Answering the question "what does it mean to understand?" can be viewed, from this perspective, as an issue of identity and awareness of one's role within the context of a broader community. Understanding goes hand in hand with the process of "becoming". If you are looking at a specific individual and want to gauge their understanding, you can explore how they identify with the community. Do they see themselves as members of that community? What role do they believe they play within that community? Do they share of the goals and ideals of that community? Do they know and engage in the practices of that community?

By exploring the practices of an individual and the meaning and role they have with respect to a broader community, we can begin to get a sense of the "understanding" of that individual. Lave and Wenger describe the mechanism of "legitimate peripheral participation" (LPP) as a crucial part of learning in a community of practice (Lave and Wenger, 1991). Initially, a member will participate in activities that are important (legitimate) to the community, but are perhaps not the central focus of that community's practices. In their example of the Vai and Gola tailors of West Africa, the novices participate legitimately by sweeping the floors of the tailor shop, but peripherally with respect to the manufacture of articles of clothing. However, they are provided with the opportunity to observe the practices and engage in the beliefs of the community. It is important to note, however, that while peripherality can be a position where access to a practice is possible, it can also be a position where outsiders are kept from moving further inward (Wenger, 1998). Lave and Wenger propose that an extended period of legitimate peripherality provides learners with opportunities to make the culture of practice their own (Lave and Wenger, 1991).

As described previously, education and learning, from a communities of practice perspective, involves " 'taking part' and 'being a part,' and both of these expressions signalize that learning should be viewed as a process of becoming a part of a greater whole (Sfard, 1998)." From this point of view, individuals who identify with a community and engage in the beliefs and practices that are important to the community demonstrate a greater degree of understanding. Individuals who participate in the periphery can be presumed to be those with a lesser degree of understanding in contrast to those who are central members.

LPP and communities of practice, as an analytical viewpoint on learning and understanding, is especially useful in learning situations that have strong social and community-oriented characteristics. In the case of learning about games, the question then becomes one of identifying the community of practice within which "understanding" will be considered. In my case, I will refer to the community of practice of game scholars and of game designers, and thus, a student's degree of understanding should be contextualized with respect to the beliefs and practices of these communities as they are currently understood and defined.

Knowledge Building

Knowledge building is a process by which ideas that are valuable to a community are continually produced and improved. For example, doctors who work on finding ways to cure cancer and engineers learning to design better engines, are all knowledge builders engaged in knowledge-building communities. Their collective goal is to advance the frontiers of knowledge as they perceive them. As they report their findings to each other and discuss their implications, they create and modify (as a community) public knowledge about their field. The result of knowledge building is the creation and modification of public knowledge-- knowledge that lives "in the world" and is available to be worked on and used by other people (Scardamalia and Bereiter, 2002).

One of the central notions of knowledge building is that knowledge is not static and certain but can be improved over time (Hill et al., 2003). Since knowledge building is a collaborative effort of multiple members of a community, it is important that participants also work on defining their shared values and goals. In particular, knowledge building is guided by a the following principles (Hill et al., 2003; van Aalst and Chan, 2007):

- Working at the cutting edge
  - Problems emerge from conflicting theories, models and findings that require further explanation
- Progressive problem solving
  - Reformulate, re-investigate and deepen understanding
- Collaborative effort
  - Importance of working on shared values and goals
- Identifying high points
  - Meta-cognitive understanding is needed for knowledge building work

However, knowledge building is not easy to achieve. In the context of traditional learning environments, for example, Bereiter (2002) points out that the main difficulty with conventional education is that students focus on understanding what has already been understood by others rather than contributing new ideas to the world. Also, the medium of knowledge building discussions may be important to achieving knowledge building's goals. It may be harder to achieve knowledge building in face to face discussion since conceptual discussions are easily left "in the air", and it is harder to use authoritative resources (Cummings, 2003). However, online discussions, in particular those that are threaded, can also be problematic since they have no systematic way of promoting convergence of ideas (Stahl, 2001). Another example of the difficulties of implementing a knowledge building environment lies in the fact that most communities require a certain critical mass of people, and knowledge-building systems require a critical mass of articulated ideas before they become useful.

Scardamalia and Bereiter explain that knowledge building is driven by discourse (1994). In particular, knowledge-building discourse focuses on problems and depths of understanding. For knowledge building, explaining is the major challenge. There must be encouragement to produce and advance theories through using them to explain increasingly diverse ideas and observations. Knowledge-building discourse is also decentralized with a focus on collective knowledge. The knowledge of those who are more advanced does not circumscribe what is to be learned or investigated while novices push discourse towards definition and clarification. Finally, knowledge-building discourse should interact productively within more broadly conceived knowledge building communities. For example, the knowledge-building that occurs in a high-school classroom should interact with that which occurs in a research institution.

In the context of games, the knowledge-building perspective highlights the importance and the characteristics that a learner's discourse should have with respect to gauging his level of understanding. Understanding can also be gauged by exploring the evolution and change of that discourse.

Moving Forward

In this chapter I have outlined what games literacy is and defined the specific aspect of games literacy that I will support: understanding games. I have also discussed the education research literature that informs how I may support learners understanding games. However, what I have described so far assumes that people interested in learning about games aren't games literate. It is reasonable to assume the opposite. After all, as I mentioned in the opening of Chapter 1, games are culturally important, and videogame playing is virtually a commonplace among those that are in a formal education environment (e.g., school and university). Are game players, for the most part, games literate? By definition, game players play games (first component of games literacy), and we can safely assume that not all of them make games (third component). However, do game players understand games (second component)? This raises the need to answer the first two questions I posed in Chapter 1: (Q1) What are the challenges of learning about games? Then, if there are indeed challenges, I can follow up with: (Q2) How do we characterize a naïve understanding of games? These questions will be explored in the next chapter. The answers to these questions will suggest further educational research literature. This literature, combined with the definitions of games literacy, games understanding, and the educational approaches I outlined in this chapter, inform the design and use of the online learning environments I will describe in Chapters 5 and 6.

CHAPTER 4: NOVICES' UNDERSTANDING OF GAMES

In Chapter 3, I established a definition for games literacy and, more specifically, what it means to understand games. However, I haven't established what the challenges are in achieving a deeper understanding of games. In this chapter I will explore two of the questions I posed earlier: (Q1) What are the challenges of learning about games?, and: (Q2) How can we characterize a naïve understanding of games? By looking at the difficulties involved in learning about games, we can gain insight into some of the needs of novice students and into how the medium of the videogame affects its study.

Methods and Data Analysis

In order to explore the challenges of learning and teaching game studies, I performed in-depth interviews with professors and instructors who teach game studies courses. In this study, I used qualitative methods to explore the diverse ways in which game studies courses are taught at the university undergraduate and graduate levels.

I take an inductive approach based on general research questions informed by game studies literature as well as some initial hypotheses. In addition to asking for details about the courses instructors teach and the challenges faced by students, my interview protocol includes open-ended questions about what changes they would make to courses, what they expect students to get out of the courses they've taught, what skills and knowledge students are expected to have to be successful in the class, and what role their prior experience with games plays in their success in the class. Instructors with extensive teaching experience are invited to comment on their experiences in general, as well as refer to specific courses they have taught recently. Interviews are semi-structured to ensure that all participants are asked certain questions yet still allow participants to raise other issues they feel are relevant to the research. The protocol includes questions such as these:

- Tell me about the assignments and class activities you had the students engage in.
- What do students have the most difficulty accomplishing?
- What can you say about the role of students' prior knowledge of games in the context of your class?

As recommended for qualitative research (Glaser and Strauss, 1967), I employ theoretical sampling in which cases are chosen based on theoretical (developed *a priori*) categories to provide polar types, rather than for statistical generalizability to a larger population (see Table 3) (Eisenhardt, 1989). I looked to interview instructors and professors from a variety of institutions of higher learning and who had some degree of experience with research in game studies. I also sought diversity in teaching experience, from those who had taught a game studies course only once to those who had taught multiple courses. Other categories covered the types and sizes of courses taught, ranging from large introductory undergraduate lecture-style courses to small advanced graduate discussion-based seminars.

Additionally, I made no attempt to provide definitions of what a "game studies course" was. When asked "Tell me about one or more game studies courses you have taught", interviewees were free to use their own understanding of the field and thus talk about courses that they feel are relevant to game studies. This helps ensure a broader range of courses, which was one of the desired goals. In the next section, I provide a sample of representative courses taught, together with their learning objectives.

Table 3: Categories and criteria for participant selection

Category	Criteria
Instructor	<Novice Instructor, Experienced Instructor> <Experienced Game Researcher, Novice Game Researcher>
Course Type	<Introductory, Advanced> <Required, Optional>
Course Style	<Lecture, Discussion, Practicum, Mixed>
Class Size	<Large: More than 30 students, Regular: Less than 30 students>
Students	<Graduate, Undergraduate, Mixed> <Homogeneous Academic Background, Heterogeneous Academic Background>

Table 4: Participant pseudonyms and class details

Instructor	Alvin	Bert	Charlie	Diane	Edward	Faye	George	Harold	Iris	Judy	Kirk	Lance
Novice Instructor			X	X						X		
Experienced Instructor	X	X			X	X	X	X	X		X	X
Novice Game Researcher			X						X			X
Experienced Game Researcher	X	X		X	X	X	X	X		X	X	
Course Type												
Introductory Course	X	X	X	X	X	X	X	X	X	X	X	X
Advanced Course	X	X		X	X	X	X					
Required Course		X	X	X	X	X	X	X	X	X	X	X
Optional Course	X				X	X		X			X	
Course Styles												
Lecture	X			X	X		X	X	X	X	X	
Discussion		X	X	X		X				X	X	
Practicum		X				X						X
Mixed					X		X					
Class Size												
Large (more than 30 students)				X	X	X			X	X	X	X
Regular (less than 30 students)	X	X	X		X	X	X	X		X	X	
Students												
Graduate	X	X		X	X	X				X		
Undergraduate	X		X	X	X	X	X	X	X	X	X	X
Mixed											X	
Homogeneous Academic Bkgd.	X		X				X				X	X
Heterogeneous Academic Bkgd.		X			X	X	X		X	X	X	

I conducted twelve interviews between August and December of 2006. Interviewees represented a total of ten institutions of higher learning from eight countries. Many interviewees reported on multiple classes. Interviews were conducted in person and by telephone, averaging 62 minutes and ranging from 35 to 74 minutes in length. All interviews were audio-recorded and transcribed. Data analysis was conducted using an iterative process, in which data from one interviewee were confirmed or contradicted by data from others, allowing me to refine theoretical categories, propositions, and conclusions as they emerged from the data (Glaser and Strauss, 1967). All interviewee names have been changed for privacy (See Table 4).

General Learning Objectives of Games Classes

Each instructor had experience with a wide variety of game courses, each with their own educational objectives and curricula. Many instructors had taught more than one course, often on more than one occasion. The following sample of representative courses, each with a brief description and outline of the main learning objectives, provides a sense of the variety of game courses being taught. The descriptions and titles of the courses have been edited for privacy reasons. Some descriptions have also been edited from multiple similar courses taught by different instructors. All of the courses described have been taught at both the undergraduate and graduate levels, and in varying class sizes. In addition to the descriptions, I also list the contexts for understanding games (see Chapter 3) that are the main focus in each of the courses.

Game Design Analysis Course

This course introduces students to the study of games as cultural artifacts and provides an initial background on the approaches to game studies that have been developed over the past ten years. At the end of this course, students are expected to have a basic understanding of the issues in game studies, what it means to study games, and what some of the fundamental questions are.

Primary foci: games in culture (first context)), games and other games (second context)

Game Design Practicum

The goal of this course is to give students a basic understanding of the challenges of creating gameplay and designing a game, and to familiarize them with the processes currently used within the games industry for creating games. In this course, students compare and re-design existing games and also work on a project where they must create their own game design, pitch it to a panel of experts, and write all the documentation necessary to guide the design process through the creation of a final game.

Primary foci: games and other games (second context), deconstruction and components (fourth context)

History and Culture of Digital Games

In this course, students study the history and culture of computer games. Students begin by learning the history of computer hardware and software, starting with early prototypes from the 1950s, continuing with arcade, console and PC games, and concluding with the current trends in online games and multimodal games. One of the goals of this course is to survey the landscape of changing games and player audiences.

Primary foci: games in culture (first context), games and other games (second context), games and technology (third context)

Theories of Games and Play

In this course, students read and discuss the work of theorists like Huizinga, Caillois, Sutton-Smith, Csikszentmihalyi and several others who have provided theoretical frameworks and interpretations on the individual meanings and social impacts of play and games. The aim is for students to participate in productive discussions of these theories as a broad framework for considering the role of play and games in our society, focusing especially on theories of digital games.

Primary focus: games in culture (first context)

Nintendo Entertainment System Course

In this course, students investigate the cultural artifacts of a computational system, in this case the Nintendo Entertainment System (NES), in concert with an analysis of its technical properties. Students play and critique a selection of NES games from the perspective of the hardware and software constraints under which they were created while also authoring original programs using emulator software. The goal of this course is to introduce students to the intimate details of the NES for the purpose of creating new games or other digital works on that system, and critiquing NES games.

Primary foci: games and other games (second context), games and technology (third context), deconstruction and components (fourth context)

Findings

Student Background

People who are interested in learning about games come from as wide a variety of academic backgrounds as researchers in game studies. Faye says, "you have computer science students, there's people who come because they love games, there's visual design students, I get a large number of film students, students from the business school, or students from any number of backgrounds, anthropology, psychology, etc." Most share an interest in games due to prior and current life experiences. This prior interest is what helps draw many students to these classes. Edward, who has a mix of art and CS students in his classes, notes that "I'd tell people about the course, and they'd get excited just out of a general interest. Games are so hot in the pop cultural sense, particularly with college students, that I was able to get a nice mix of students into the class."

Many students also register for these classes because they aspire to work in the games industry. Lance describes how "they're here because when they come out [graduate], they want to work on games." Other students, especially at the higher levels of education, want to complement their already games-related professional lives. Some are professional game designers, journalists, or musicians with years of practical experience. For them, applying to games-related programs or taking games classes is a way of "linking their passion and expertise in games with what they do professionally" says Bert.

Perhaps surprisingly, some do not have what we would call a formal education. Judy describes her experience: "I'm teaching a masters course and I've got a really big diversity of people in the course. Some people have only worked in industry and haven't done an undergraduate program. Other people have come from art programs. There's a woman who's just finished a degree in English at Yale, another guy comes from acoustic engineering, and a few people come from computing backgrounds." Lance's experience in his undergraduate classes is similar, "90% of them are high school graduates. The other 10% are usually people who, for whatever reason, didn't go to school or something like that. All of a sudden they've decided to come back to school. They're much older, like 40 or 45."

The most common differentiator, especially at the undergraduate level, is the academic background of the students. Most often, students come from technical backgrounds (computer science, engineering) or the humanities (media studies, art, or film). Iris says, "Generally, they come from science and engineering backgrounds, including computer science, as well as other areas. Every other semester I'll get a big group of humanities majors. These last few semesters have been more balanced, and I've been told that word is getting out that I teach a lot of videogames stuff in my class, and people are just signing up."

What effect does this variety of interests, background and expertise play in the context of a single course? First, it makes it harder to establish a common level of academic discourse in the class. When you have people with different backgrounds, the common denominator becomes quite low. Harold describes the issue as "if I try to make it very basic, then, of course, some people would be bored and find the level too low. Half the class wants one thing, and the other wants another. It can be quite frustrating for all parties involved." Judy describes this challenge as "I find that I have to outline basic theories. I'm sort of providing a basic toolbox that I wouldn't have to do if they had all come from similar backgrounds. The ones that know that, well, they sort of get frustrated."

On the other hand, particularly in design-focused classes, the heterogeneity of the students provides them opportunities to experience different perspectives and move away from their areas of familiarity. Kirk notes that "everyone has a certain background, whether it's computing, or visual design, or something else, like a literary background, or what have you. They all have different interests, goals, and also different trajectories. So there's a kind of a richness of different texture that they bring. These differences often create conflict. This is great because we can have actual conversations about those issues and show them [the students] that reconciliation is actually not the goal." Also, student heterogeneity can allow them to bring multiple skills to bear in their design projects and practice the communicational and management skills that will be useful to them in the workplace.

Role of Prior Experience with Videogames

Literature in education and learning has highlighted the important role that prior experience can play in learning (Lave and Wenger, 1991; Bransford et al., 2000; Kolodner and Guzdial, 2000). In particular, it is important to establish personally meaningful connections with what is to be learned (Papert, 1980). For example, the creation and design of games, considered personally meaningful to kids, has been explored as a productive means for learning computer programming (Kafai, 1995; Bruckman, 2000). I hypothesized that students' extensive personal histories with videogames would be an asset in learning about games.

My results suggest that prior experience with videogames can have a positive effect in the students' motivation, commitment and dedication. Charlie describes how "they realized that their passion could transform into something more serious. Even if they do not want to be involved in game studies or industry, they realized that gaming is not just for nerds, or for losing time, but something that deserved particular attention." Also, students' personal game histories provided them with a rich source of knowledge to draw from.

> *"[Students] regularly come up with really good examples that aren't discussed in any of the class materials. They rely on their own experiences, memories, and the expert knowledge they have of some genres. They can highlight the complexities that are involved in an issue rather than have this kind of uniform understanding of some received wisdom. We regularly ended up with this kind of varied and multicolored idea of the multiple points of view related to all the various aspects of games, their features, their role in social life, culture and so on."* **– Bert**

However, many respondents reported that the role of personal game playing experience, especially when it was significant, was often negative.

> *"Their personal experience with games is actually a hindrance. It would be far better if they were coming at it without any experience in games. I find that what I do most is peel away what they already think they know from playing these previous games. So that's the biggest problem: peeling that 'knowledge' away."* **– Lance**

In many ways, being expert videogame players interferes with their abilities to step back from their role as "gamers" or "fans" and reason critically and analytically about the games they are studying or designing. As Diane describes, "it's hard for them to break out of being a fan. It's even that much harder to take an objective step back, because they just have so much fun playing games." Edward comments that, "it's harder for them to step back objectively and get past the [idea that] I like games, I like to approach it as a fan, I wanna like a game… anything else either doesn't interest them or they can't seem to get around it."

> *"Students who know every game often have preconceptions about what games are, and I have to break those preconceptions. I have to find ways to make them see that games are an aesthetic form that hasn't been exhausted. Just because these are certain games or genres in existence, and this is the way things are... This is not the only way it can be! And so, breaking that down is*

sometimes more difficult than starting from scratch with someone who's maybe a casual gamer or just curious"   **– Faye**

Students also find it harder to accept new ideas about games when their judgments are clouded by false assumptions about particular genres, titles and even the era a game is from. For example, they often assume that an Atari 2600 game, due to its simplicity in graphics and archaic hardware platform[8], isn't worthy of in-depth analysis or can't have any artistic or cultural meaning. Kirk describes how, "I think that students often have issues with the conceptual idea of playing, let's say, a vintage arcade game carefully. The very notion that there's something in there, more than they can see from a single glance, is much more difficult for them than, say, admitting that Grand Theft Auto has some subtleties of meaning that they could tease out." For students, the apparent complexity of a game and the meaning they might be able to tease out often seem at odds.

Students are also challenged by having to shift from treating a game as a "consumer media good" to a cultural artifact that can have embedded meaning and ideas. Playing a game as a child over countless weekends with your friends creates a strong and lasting emotional experience that is difficult to overcome. Games that have been played in the past are viewed with nostalgia, and students have to come to terms with, in Alvin's words, "separating the memories of the good old times they had with the harsh reality that 90% of retro games are just rubbish."

The diversity of the prior videogame experience students have also plays an important role. Harold comments that "they [students] don't know enough about games when they start studying games. They don't know enough about the history of games, not only computer games, but other types of games as well. One way of putting it is that they haven't played enough games, to be more precise, they haven't played enough different types of games." While students often have over ten years of experience playing videogames, that experience can be limited in diversity. It is typical for students to have a specialized understanding of a particular game genre, like first-person shooters, but be completely ignorant, in terms of experience, of other genres like puzzle or sports games. George describes that "there are often people in my classes who have just played one genre of games. Maybe they've only played tabletop role-playing games, or maybe its just first person shooters and nothing else. These students have problems in the course because they can't relate to a lot of the material." These students' knowledge and experience is so ingrained in particular genre conventions, that taking alternate viewpoints

---

[8]   The Atari 2600 is a video game console released in 1977 that featured a microprocessor and popularized the use of cartridges that contained game code. It was a commercial success in the late 1970's and early 1980's. (Perry and Wallich,1983)

and discussing other phenomena becomes much harder. This difficulty is often met by students with disbelief and strong emotional reactions. Lance describes how students "actually get angry, 'cause they think that

they know games. They really get confused, angry, and frustrated, because they've been playing games all their life!"

Students often react by antagonizing the instructor when faced with the thought that they may not be as well-educated as they thought. As Iris describes, "some of them are convinced that they already *know* videogames. They already have an opinion and you can't teach them anything about a game they already played. In their minds, they're already experts. Their attitude is that you can't correct me." Students also question their teachers' gaming credentials: Who are you to tell me this? What games did you design? Have you played all the games I have? What games do you know?

Sometimes student's attitudes can also negatively affect their relationship towards the university itself. Instead of being a place where they can learn, the university course simply becomes a necessary step in the process of getting a diploma or a means for learning specific software tools they think are needed to get a job. In their minds, they are already qualified to work in the game industry, and everything else simply becomes an obstacle towards meeting that goal. As Lance mentions, "they think they already know how to make the best first person shooter or the best strategy game. So, their attitude is to demand that I just show them the 3D tools so they can start making them."

Edward's experience is similar "I've noticed that in the last five or six years students come in with a sense of entitlement. They treat their games education like a service and they're the customers. Their attitude is very much like 'I pay tuition. That doesn't mean that I'm a student, it means you should give me what I want'. This can get complicated when you need to push them in a different way, which can be quite often with students in [the program] I teach."

Practices and Discourse of Play

A lot of experience with videogames can also help confuse two issues: playing for fun and entertainment with playing for critical analysis and understanding. Kirk describes how "[students] mistake being successful at the play of the game, being a good player, as being a clever player...or a player with insight. The ability to perform in the game is not the same as being able to read or think about the game carefully." For some students, analyzing a game is equivalent to listing all its features together with their opinion: is it cool or not? "A lot of times people, when they get right down to it, sort of slip into feature reviews. It's one of the most difficult things to break, that kind of loose judgment on whether something is working or not", says Faye. George provides additional insight "If they're comparing two games, for example, they usually haven't thought out the reasons why they want to compare them. So, what they do is take two games they like, and then they just describe them. If you're lucky, they might tell you why they are like each other, and why they are different from each other. But they don't have a purpose for it, they just do it mechanically."

Edward describes how new modes of playing and thinking about games "sort of pushes them [the students] out of their comfort zone. I really wanted them to think more critically and to really push them to do it in a standard academic way. They really struggled with that. It was a masters level course, and I still had to really push them to work on their critical analysis." I found that it is common for students to have problems expressing ideas about gameplay or articulating their experience with games.

My research suggests that students are generally lacking in models of what an in-depth analysis or a game critique look like. Diane describes that "they might have opinions about things, and they are often extremely valid and interesting opinions, but it's also difficult for them to square that with using a methodological framework for thinking about a particular problem or addressing a certain issue." Judy mentions that students will typically "write reviews, so they say this is a really good game. I think that that's because most of the things that they've read have been games journalism, so they're kind of following that mode." Unfortunately, game reviews, which are written to help consumers decide whether or not they want to purchase a certain game (Stuart, 2005; Klostermann, 2006), are a poor referent for the kinds of in-depth analysis and critique which are often expected of students studying games. Ernest Adams, a professional game designer and consultant, comments that "reviews only compare games to other games; they don't analyze games in their larger cultural context (Friedl, 2002)."

While students often have a very good feel for gameplay aspects, they can have difficulties articulating what these aspects are and how they interact with each other to produce a game experience. Edward describes "they're very savvy about picking up a controller and figuring out how to play a game pretty much instantaneously. They get the general, 'Oh, here's how you interact with this game', and they can do that immediately. Sometimes it's magical watching them do it. So, that learning curve has already been attained just by their history playing games. That unbelievable familiarity makes them experts, but what's interesting is when you ask them to talk about games. They kind of devolve into likes and dislikes. So, they'll say things like, 'I played this game and I liked it because...' or 'I really enjoyed the…'. Understanding what they're trying to say gets really muddy because there is no sense of exactly what they're saying outside of that they like it, or don't like it." Faye describes the issue as one of lack of vocabulary.

> *"We don't have a strong vocabulary for understanding what happens when you play. It's difficult to open up emotionally and describe what you feel. We experience games at a very visceral level and don't have, as a culture, a strong literacy in discussing games. You might go to a movie and someone who's not a filmmaker can discuss with you, at a deep level, the character motivations, or the editing of the film. The same can't really be said about gameplay. People can discuss the technology, but that's not what I'm interested in. I'm interested in how gameplay affects the human being, how the emotional experience is playing out."*
> **– Faye**

Faye's comment raises another issue. Are these challenges unique to students studying games? Alvin mentions some of the differences he sees between film analysis and game analysis assignments. In his view, the idea that you can talk about games in a serious and academic fashion hasn't really moved beyond academia. Thus, students aren't aware of what "appropriate" models of discourse surrounding games are, and end up writing in the same style as what they read.

> *"When I force them to write a game analysis, students often fall back into a style that I call talking about 'the fun world of games.' Basically, it's really horrible writing about games. A lot of journalistic writing about games is like this. Students think they can get away with the same level of analysis that they get from these publications. They'll write stuff saying, 'You have a really big gun that is pretty cool and shiny'. This even happens with the grad students! When I give the same assignment for film analysis, the results are different. People know that you could fill five libraries with books about film analysis. Students know they can't just analyze a scene by saying, 'he comes from the left, and then he shoots the guy to the right, and it's really cool how he does that!' You don't do this in a film analysis, and students are aware of this tradition. In the case of games, the publications they read very often do that, so this carries over towards the analysis."* -
> **Alvin**

So, in what ways do course instructors deal with these challenges of lack of critical vocabulary and appropriate models of discourse, problems articulating ideas and insights, and the challenge of playing games for analysis and critique rather than fun? Course instructors have adopted a variety of approaches to help students engage in the sort of discourse that is expected. George describes, "I provide a vocabulary and framework for games, both game design patterns and the game ontology project[9], so that they can look at a game and see the kinds of parts which are used when you describe what happens during a game, what are the structural components in a game, and so on." Charlie, who also uses game design patterns and the Game Ontology (Björk and Holopainen, 2005; Zagal et al., 2005), illustrates, "with these tools they recognize things that they might know, and then transform their language together with their comprehension of games." Prior to this study, I was not aware that Charlie and George used the Game Ontology in their classes. Their reasons for doing so, providing students with access to vocabulary and concepts, suggests that the Ontology can be a valuable learning resource for students as will be explored further in Chapter 6.

Students are also often asked to write journals or take notes of their experiences playing games. These self-reflective, often story-telling, experiences help students, in Faye's words, "get into their emotional state and try to understand what they're feeling and thinking." Also, as Judy points out, "they [students] can begin to illustrate an argument or analysis with concrete examples of how a particular aspect of something is managed. Instead of going into a generality about a game, they are thinking about it in more specific details." The use of note-taking and writing journals for supporting learning about games will be explored further in Chapter 5.

Issues of the Medium

Fully experiencing a videogame is comparable to being skillful at playing it. Can you push the buttons fast enough to gain access to the final area? Iris describes how a student once confided, "I no longer play videogames because I don't understand the controls. Give me a NES[10] controller any day, but these new ones with all those buttons? I don't know what to do with so many buttons!"

"The idea of being good at something, especially in a videogame, where we don't really have random access to every page, we can't skip around, means that in some games there may be certain aspects of the game that are unavailable to you. You know, unless we use saves or all these sorts of tricks that we can

---

[9] Game design patterns and the game ontology project (www.gameontology.org) are frameworks that provide concepts and vocabulary for describing and analyzing structural elements of games and how they relate to each other. Further details in Chapter 6.
[10] NES refers to the Nintendo Entertainment System. It was released in the United States in 1985.

use to see parts of the game. But you might, whether through frustration or just through inability, not really unlock the game's secrets...even if you're very adept at uncovering them once you find them." – **Kirk**

This problem of access poses a challenge to students and instructors on multiple levels. Students who are unfamiliar with a particular game have to acquire and practice the skills necessary to be proficient at it. This entry barrier makes it harder to establish a common reference point for all the learners in a class.

Harold describes his experience with a student unfamiliar with first-person shooters, "We were playing Counter Strike, and it was painfully clear that [the student] did not know anything about how the game worked, or how any first person shooter works."

While you could assume that most students are familiar with first-person shooters, the same cannot be said of other genres. The breadth of games, despite their potential value as objects of study, becomes limited by their exclusion due to lack of students' familiarity with them. Also, playing games is time-consuming, and often, playing all the games that are assigned in a class is simply impossible. George describes how he "In order for them to do their assignments in the amount of time they have in the course, they really need to understand the game. So, I encourage them to choose games they've already played. The course isn't long enough for them to have time to go home and play a game sufficiently to be able to analyze it. So, at least in this class, there's a general assumption that if you're taking a game related course you're supposed to know about games or played a lot of games before." For other classes, where the educational objectives may include exposing the students to certain games they may not otherwise know, the issue becomes more complicated.

"Say you have twenty different games you want the class to have exposure to. Now imagine how many hours of play that would take!" – **Judy**

There is no easy solution. Some classes take a broad, yet shallow, approach where it is assumed that the students will play all the games, though none for very long. In other cases, individual students are nominated as the "expert" for a particular game. They are expected to devote a significant amount of time to playing and understanding a particular game. Then they give a presentation, including a demo, of important aspects of the game. Some classes implicitly assume that students are already experienced and intimately familiar with the games that will be studied.

Technology can also play a problematic role when studying games.

"It's really difficult to teach a class across the spectrum of historical platforms and the evolution of interface languages. I mean, it's just difficult to make sure that you have a working version of the original Super Mario Brothers when you only have one and I have to bring in my own machine to play it. The lab doesn't, you know, have every old game console available." – **Faye**

The problem of providing students with access to games that are important to the history of videogames is not about curiosity or nostalgia. As Edward describes in the context of his game design class, "We're having to consider going back so that they don't re-invent the wheel every time they think of a game design or how a game could work. It's about knowing what has been done or also, what good experiments and innovations have occurred."

These difficulties often lead to students blindly pursuing ideas that have historically proven ineffective or impoverish their chances of capitalizing and building on prior knowledge and experience.

Role and Influence of the Field of Game Studies

Most of the study participants reported difficulties wrestling with what "the basics" of an introductory game studies course should be. As Kirk puts it, "If you look around at the world of introductory game studies classes, you'd find that while they may share publications, all of them are all over the map". There was also genuine curiosity of what other instructors were doing, what pedagogical techniques had proven valuable, and how they dealt with the challenges they faced.

Bert poses a fundamental question: "Do we really have enough research in this field [game studies] that our teaching has some solid foundation?" Other fields, with hundreds of years of research, have figured out, to a certain extent, what the fundamentals are. In the case of game studies, instructors are figuring out what to borrow from fields like media studies, sociology, and social psychology among others. At the same time, so many new phenomena are emerging that while they're teaching, they're doing research. Despite the challenges, teaching game studies was reported as fruitful and rewarding.

In what ways does the relative youth of the field influence the students who are learning about games?

"Film analysis has all kinds of references. Game analysis is a bit less clear. There are maybe two or three books that might be references, but the context is still growing. You can't stand on the shoulders of giants in game research. There's missing work that hasn't been done yet, and that makes it harder for the students to contextualize what they do." – **Alvin**

The field's lack of established canon can be problematic for some students, particularly those from science or engineering backgrounds. They often expect to encounter problems with clear-cut solutions. Instead, they face a field whose fundamental questions are still being explored. George describes that "the most common question I get about the assignments is that the task they're given is not well defined. They have a problem with them because the questions are so open. This is actually frightening to some people, because then they don't know if what they're doing is good, or bad. They're used to doing something, and being able to immediately determine if it's wrong." Diane provides an example, "we spend some time talking about the ludology versus narratology question, and some students wonder why we bother. Like, isn't this resolved? They think that problems get solved and we move through them, and I don't know that any problems have really been solved."

"Game studies has been such a self-reflexive field that it further problematizes this issue. When someone writes an article about how they shouldn't write an article about something, it can be disorienting for the new student who doesn't really understand where the field is at." – **Kirk**

While engaging in a new field can be daunting for students, it also provides a unique opportunity. Bert describes that "people feel this pioneer spirit. It's not only students, but also we, as teachers, are pretty excited about being able to go into this field and speak about games. It's very exciting to go where no one in our university has gone before". Contrary to other fields, students feel greater liberty to question and criticize what they read and learn. As students come to terms with the fact that game studies is new, they often engage in the dialectic and fluid nature of the field.

"They have this tremendous opportunity to play a central role. This is a ridiculously new field that's quite accessible for participation and even publication. Most of the time, in a class, you wouldn't have direct access to the top scholarship. They have that opportunity! They just have to want to do it." – **Kirk**

The state of the field, together with a positive affective relationship with games, is a determining factor in the high motivation that students often show. Charlie reports that his students are often self-motivated to "start reading a lot of essays about game studies, even if they were in English or in other languages they didn't know. Every week we discovered some new authors and engaged their ideas with a lot of passion."

Characterizing a Naïve Understanding of Videogames

Answering my second question, (Q2) How can we characterize a naïve understanding of games?, can help us design better learning environments to support learners. My analysis shows that we can take a first step towards characterizing what a naïve understanding of games is. Summarizing, someone with a naïve understanding of games will often:

1. Confuse being insightful about a game with being successful at playing a game.
2. Describe a game superficially.
   - Focus on the features of a game over describing the rhetoric of a game or the experience of playing it (e.g. "this game has hi-res graphics", "the game has a ton of maps to play").
   - Describe a game judgmentally rather than analytically (e.g., "this game sucks", "this game is cool").
3. Assume that people experience a game the same way they do.
4. Be familiar with specific genres or types of games, but have a narrow view of the medium.
5. Think they can't learn anything new from games they've already played.

Discussion

Where education is concerned, games can be motivating when it comes to learning (Malone, 1981). However, it is dangerous to assume that learning will be easy, fun, or happen felicitously simply because the subject matter is games. Research has shown that when using commercial games for educational purposes, motivation and fun only go so far. There is a need to spend significant amounts of time becoming experienced with the game before any of the "learning" can actually start to happen (Squire, 2005).

Challenges of learning about games

In answer to my first question: (Q1) What are the challenges of learning about games?, my analysis shows that teaching and learning about games can be challenging for multiple reasons. Often, the extensive prior experience students have with games is counter-productive to their learning goals. Students often have problems stepping back and viewing the medium critically. Also, while they may have a specialized understanding of a particular game genre, they are often ignorant of other genres. Their knowledge is ingrained in particular genre conventions, and taking alternate viewpoints and discussing other phenomena becomes much harder. Essentially, they are challenged by having to shift from treating a game as a "consumer media good" to a cultural artifact that can have embedded meaning and ideas. This often results in students confusing playing for fun and entertainment (as "gamers") with playing for critical analysis and understanding (as future designers or game scholars). In this way students often mistake being successful at the play of the game, with being a player with insight.

Learning and teaching games can also be challenging due to the medium itself. Playing games is time-consuming and students who are unfamiliar with a particular game have to acquire and practice the skills necessary to be proficient at it. Fully experiencing a videogame is comparable to being skillful at playing it, thus studying games can create an entry barrier that makes it harder to establish a common reference point for all the learners in a class, or exclude students who aren't able to master the skills necessary to be sufficiently successful at a game. The rapid evolution of technological platforms used to play games also conspires against the study of games. As platforms become obsolete, it becomes increasingly challenging to provide students with access to games that are important to the history of videogames. Also, student judgment can be clouded by false assumptions and nostalgia. Old games with simple graphics aren't necessarily simple games, a point that is often lost on students.

Novice Players and Gamers

My research also suggests that there may be important differences, in terms of challenges faced, by students that are novices to games and those that are identify themselves as "fans" or "gamers". Students who don't have much prior experience playing games generally seem to face two main challenges: (1) issues of accessibility to the medium, and (2) assumptions of prior gameplay experience on the part of course instructors. Depending on the course, these challenges may not be an issue. For example, in courses where instructors provide time for students to familiarize themselves with the games they're expected to learn about. Students that are "fans" or "gamers", however face a different set of challenges. The main challenges faced by "gamers" can be summarized as: (1) Difficulties stepping back from role of "gamers", (2) problems articulating and describing gameplay, (3) problems assuming different viewpoints and perspectives on games. There are, as described earlier, other issues that may apply to both types of students, or even differently amongst the same types. For instance, some "gamers" may have broader experience with games than others, thus potentially having less issues assuming different viewpoints and perspectives on games. It is also possible to "level the playing field" between non-gamers and gamers by encouraging students to play games from genres they aren't familiar with. However, in order to better address these questions, further research would be required.

Addressing the Challenges of Learning About Games

Professors and instructors are actively exploring ways to overcome the difficulties students face when learning about games. Encouraging students to keep journals of their gameplaying activities seems to help them better reflect on the nature of games as well as encourage articulation of their experiences and observations. I will explore this idea further in Chapter 5 in the context of GameLog, an online environment to support reflective gameplay. Providing students with theoretical frameworks for the discussion of games seems to help improve the quality of game analyses as well as enrich their vocabulary. I will explore this idea further in Chapter 6, using the Game Ontology Project. Finally, in-class game playing sessions and in-depth presentations of games can help broaden students' experience. Although these results are encouraging, further research is still necessary. For example, it is not clear how critical experience in other media, like film or literature, may transfer to understanding games. How is this sort of experience useful? How do we help students better leverage their personal videogame experiences and help them step away from their role as "gamers" towards one of game scholars? These are questions that I will explore in the following chapters in the context of two different online environments: GameLog and the Game Ontology Wiki.

I also found that, due to the challenges posed by the medium, many classes make assumptions about the game experience of incoming students. Students are expected to be intimately familiar with a lot of the games they will study because there isn't enough time in class to play or analyze them. This assumption could have unintended effects on the diversity of people who could become future members of the field. Implicitly requiring incoming students to have years of experience with certain genres of games marginalizes those who don't. When it comes to learning about games, what should be taken for granted and what should not? Should game scholars be required to have been previously gamers?

Summarizing, this chapter explores the two first questions posed: (Q1) What are the challenges of learning about games?, and (Q2) characterize a naïve understanding of games?. The answers to these questions are discussed in the context of the results of a study that explores the issues and challenges faced by instructors of game studies classes. Using a semi-structured protocol, I interviewed twelve professors and instructors of game studies courses. The interviews were transcribed and iteratively coded to identify and refine theoretical categories, propositions and conclusions. My results indicate that learning about games can be challenging for multiple reasons. Findings include:

- Extensive prior videogame experience often interferes with students' abilities to reason critically and analytically about games.

- Students have difficulties articulating their experiences and observations.

- The medium itself presents obstacles to access. Students must be skilled at games to fully experience them.

- Technological barriers make it difficult for students to experience older games.

CHAPTER 5: SUPPORTING UNDERSTANDING THROUGH BLOGGING

In many game classes, students are asked to think about and reflect on their understanding as they play, analyze, and think critically about the games they play. I showed earlier that this is something students in games classes find challenging. Students often confuse being insightful about a game with being successful at playing it. When describing a game, students also tend to focus on issues that aren't interesting or relevant to the learning objectives of the class they are in. For example, they might describe a game superficially, focusing on the features of a game or describing it judgmentally instead of analytically.

One way of thinking about these issues is to frame them in the context of how these students play games. Essentially, how can we help students shift their mode of play from one of "gamers" or "fans" towards one of "game designers" or "game scholars?"

In this chapter, I will begin to explore the third question I posed: (Q3) How can we help students leverage knowledge from personal experiences with games to create abstract and deeper knowledge? I explore one possible way to answer this question: How can using GameLog, an online blog of gameplay experiences, support reflective game playing and, thus, a deeper understanding of videogames. In this way, I aim to help students get more from their experiences with games

Blogging for Learning

As a theory of learning, constructivism posits that learning is a process of building and refining knowledge structures. Knowledge cannot simply be transmitted; rather knowledge is constructed or created by learners as they build their own cognitive structures or mental models (Piaget, 1972). In this context, writing can be a powerful tool for constructing new knowledge (Forte and Bruckman, 2006). Research has long suggested that writing can empower learners to reflect on what they know and integrate existing knowledge with new knowledge (Britton et al., 1975; Emig, 1977; Bereiter and Scardamalia, 1987).

There are many different ways in which writing activities have been successfully used for learning. However, we are interested in one in particular: the learning log. Learning logs are written responses to learning where students reflect on their understanding, thoughts, and ideas about their study (Baker, 2003). Learning logs are used to stimulate metacognitive awareness in learners and meta-cognition itself is a challenging skill that

61

must be learned and practiced (Barron et al., 1998; Bransford et al., 2000). However, by keeping learning logs, students can assume responsibility for and take command of their learning (Commander and Smith, 1996). Traditionally, learning logs are paper based. However, in the form of weblogs or blogs, educators have also begun experimenting with taking learning logs online (Stiler and Philleo, 2003; Reagin, 2004; Wiltse, 2004; Du and Wagner, 2005). Wiltse, for example, studied journalism students who used a blog to summarize and reflect on the daily student presentations they attended in class. Student blog entries were supposed to include a summary of the topic and the student's reaction to it, such as whether they learned something new or surprising (Wiltse, 2004).

A blog is a user-generated website where entries are made in journal style and displayed in reverse chronological order. They are generally publicly readable and, by allowing visitors to post comments, allow for limited asynchronous interaction. Research has shown that, among other things, people are motivated to write blogs to express themselves, as an outlet for thoughts and feelings, as a way to think by writing, and to foster community (Nardi et al., 2004).

In the context of learning, and in addition to the effects of paper-based learning logs, blogging offers possibilities for collaborative learning by allowing learners to share knowledge and experience with each other. Additionally, learners can be exposed to a diversity of perspectives and interact with each other in constructive ways.

The personal nature of a blog together with its public nature is also aligned with the idea that people learn better through building personally meaningful artifacts and sharing them with others (Papert, 1991). Some authors have also proposed that the public nature of blogging can help students develop an understanding that writing is a social and collaborative process rather than the act of an individual in solitary (Walker, 2005).

In the following section, I introduce GameLog, a custom developed online blogging environment designed for learners to engage in reflective practices of their gameplaying activities.

I consider it a domain-specific kind of online learning log designed to, among other things, help people think about their experiences with games, achieve a deeper understanding of games, establish connections across games, identify structural gameplay elements in multiple games, understand how gameplay can evolve and change over the course of a game, and articulate the emotional and personally meaningful experiences they have while playing.

GameLog

GameLog is a publicly accessible online community where people keep track of the videogames they are playing as well as those they have played (available at http://www.gamelog.cl). GameLog's primary feature is to allow registered users to write a blog of their gameplaying experience for each game they play. It is different from traditional blogging environments in that each user maintains multiple parallel blogs. Each GameLog is devoted to a particular game. When a user starts playing a new game, he creates a GameLog for that game and can then write his thoughts and feelings about it. When done playing, he can "close" his GameLog and indicate the reasons for closing the GameLog.

Figure 1 shows a few GameLogs created by a user. As indicated by the "Finished" status, this user's GameLog for *The Sims* is currently closed. The GameLogs for *Grand Theft Auto–San Andreas* and *Zelda: Windwaker*, are also closed, but the user has indicated more information about why he is no longer playing them. Despite being closed, all three GameLogs are still available for public reading. The GameLog for *The Sims 2*, is marked as "Playing", indicating that it is an active, or open, GameLog.

	's GameLogs	
	has been with GameLog for **0** years. **4** months, and **5** days	
	Game	Status/Read GameLog
1	Grand Theft Auto - San Andreas (PS2)	Stopped playing - Something better came along
2	The Sims (PC)	Finished playing
3	The Sims 2 (PC)	Playing
4	Zelda: Windwaker (GC)	Stopped playing - Technical problems

Figure 1: List of GameLogs (user has been anonymized)

For each open GameLog, the owner can write an unlimited number of individual posts or entries. Each entry also includes the date and time written, when it was last edited and the number of total edits made since it was posted. In traditional blog manner, when viewing a GameLog, entries are displayed in reverse-chronological order. Users, including the owner, are allowed to write follow-up comments to each post. Table 5 shows a fragment of a post written for a particular GameLog. Whenever someone writes a comment on an entry, the owner of the GameLog is notified via e-mail and provided with a link to reply. The site also offers basic search and browsing functionality to allow users to find GameLogs written for particular games or by other users.

Table 5: GameLog excerpt
(Legend of Zelda: The Wind Waker)

November 19, 2006 10:20:48 AM
I went exploring again in Wind Waker, mainly to fill in some of the spots on Link's map. After a while, I came across one of the huge whirlwinds and fought the critter on a cloud inside of it. Even though it made it rather hard to aim at the critter properly, I really like the fact that the winds from the tornado affected the arrows Link shot off. Really, wind seems to be implemented better/more in this game than most others... which is appropriate, considering its theme. I just wish more games with weather effects -had- actually effects from the weather, not just pretty graphics. (Not that I object to pretty graphics.) After beating the cloud-guy...

Study

In Fall of 2006, GameLog was used as part of the regular curriculum in two game classes taught by the same instructor at a local university. The first class was an undergraduate lecture-style class where students explored and analyzed key developments in the history of digital media (U-class). While videogames were a significant part of the curriculum, students also learned about virtual environments, interactive television, the world wide web, and artificial intelligence for interactive characters. The second class I studied was a mixed graduate and undergraduate discussion-based class where students debated and engaged in issues of game design and analysis as a cultural practice (G-class). In this class students also explored game genres and their representational goals. In both classes, students were required, as part of their regular coursework, to play and design games, read scholarly articles, and turn in written assignments.

As part of their regular coursework, students in both classes were asked to keep a GameLog and write about their experiences playing a game chosen from a list of assigned games for that class. For the U-class, students were asked to choose one game, while they had to choose three games in the G-class. In both classes students were asked to play the game on at least three different occasions for at least 30 minutes each time. For each time they played the game, they were asked to write a GameLog entry. The assignment asked them to write about the experience they had while playing the game, including their thoughts on the characters, narrative and gameplay (characters and story, for the U-class). Also, in the case of the undergraduate class, students were asked to submit a short response summarizing their experience with GameLog. These responses were also collected and analyzed. The students' GameLog entries were not graded in the U-Class, though they were assessed on the quality of the short responses they submitted. In the case of the G-Class, students were graded on their completion of the assignment, not on the content of their written GameLog entries. The duration of the assignment was officially one week, although students were encouraged to begin their GameLog activities sooner.

Student Impressions

In order to get a sense of the students' perceptions of the GameLog assignment, together with the role they felt it played in their educational experience I conducted eight in-depth interviews once both classes had concluded. Three interviewees were chosen from the U-class and four from the G-class, in addition to the course instructor. As recommended for qualitative research (Glaser and Strauss, 1967), I employ theoretical sampling in which cases are chosen based on theoretical (developed a priori) categories to provide polar types, rather than for statistical generalizability to a larger population (Eisenhardt, 1989). Interview subjects were selected based on their academic level (undergraduate, graduate), level of interest displayed during class (engaged, not engaged), and participation on GameLog (minimum required, active participation).

Interviews were conducted in person and by telephone, averaging 46 minutes and ranging from 22 to 82 minutes in length. In addition to asking students about their experience using GameLog, the interview protocol includes questions about potential challenges of learning about games. The answers to these questions corroborate data described in Chapter 4. The student protocol also includes open-ended questions about their expectations regarding the course and changes they would make to the assignments. Interviews were semi-structured to ensure that all participants were asked certain questions yet still allow them to raise other issues they felt were relevant to the research. In the case of the students in the U-Class, I was able to use their written responses as prompts for additional questions and topics of interest.

All the interviews were audio-recorded and transcribed. I then analyzed and coded them in an iterative process to identify and refine theoretical categories, propositions, and conclusions as they emerged from the data (Glaser and Strauss, 1967). I was interested in understanding what impressions students had of the GameLog assignment and what role they felt the assignment played in the context of their learning. Would students find it a meaningful and useful experience and if so, in what ways? Would they find that it detracted from their experience of playing games (i.e., turn the experience of playing games from "fun" into "an academic chore")? My analysis would hopefully show evidence of the role the GameLog assignment played in helping students achieve a deeper understanding of games. The interviews were also used to help contextualize students' GameLog entries. For example, I was interested in understanding how they went about writing their GameLog entries, why they chose to write what they wrote, what role they felt their peers' played in this process, and so on. The results of my analysis of students' GameLogs entries follow in later sections.

For my analysis, I used open coding to bring themes to the surface from deep inside the data (Neuman, 2000). In this process I assigned codes or labels to each interview answer. These codes or labels often overlapped, and individual interview answers often had more than one code or label assigned. Sometimes, as in the case of lengthy interview responses, I assigned different codes to different parts of each response. As I analyzed each interview, new codes emerged and existing ones were modified. This process continued until no further codes emerged. As part of this process I was also looking to identify consistencies between codes (codes with similar meanings or pointing to the same basic idea) that would begin to reveal themes.

In terms of the results of my analysis, I found that students generally responded favorably to the GameLog assignment. This contradicted the feedback that the instructor reported receiving prior to the completion of the assignment. He commented that "the students complained. Not all of them, but some of them. [...] I think that the complaint had to do with the feeling that there was an exercise that they were performing whose value they could not immediately judge. Why am I doing this?" My interview data shows that, once the assignment had ended, students perceived writing GameLogs as a positive learning experience. They reported the experience as interesting and enjoyable and remarked on its utility to them from an educational perspective. Aaron felt that "this written assignment is the best one so far", while Benjamin comments that it was "an interesting and productive experience." Cynthia summarizes the general impression of the students: "I found that writing journal entries about my game play was quite fun." I found that students attributed their positive impression of the experience of blogging about their gameplay experiences to three reasons:

1. Improves relationship with videogames as a medium
2. Provides a vehicle for expression, communication, and collaboration
3. Facilitates deeper understanding of videogames

In the following sub-sections I will discuss each of these reasons with supporting evidence and, where appropriate, I will also describe how my observations and findings illustrate students' understanding of videogames according to the four contexts for understanding games that I defined in Chapter 3.

Improved Relationship with Videogames

For the most part, students in both the graduate and undergraduate classes have had extensive personal experience with videogames, which are an important part of their everyday lives. Videogames are a medium they enjoy and are familiar with. This corroborates the results of a prior study that found that among college students "gaming is virtually commonplace. Computer, video and online games are woven into the fabric of everyday life for college students (Jones, 2003)". Many students commented about how the experience of writing about the games they played improved their enjoyment of games in general. Dominic describes that "writing my GameLog allowed me to work through my gaming experience. […] I was able to get a deeper appreciation for the game that I was playing." Ellen doesn't consider herself a gamer and wrote about a game she had never played before. Like others, she noted, "I thought it was an interesting way to approach playing videogames because this helped me understand how I was playing and what I was doing. I think that now, when I actually play games, if I approach the game a different way, maybe I would enjoy playing games more, or I would have a better time." During their experience with GameLog, students begin to realize that engaging with the medium of videogames is an active process requiring more than "merely" playing. In addition to playing, they also reflected on how they were playing, what their expectations were, and what they felt when playing. As I will describe later, they also began to change the way they played games. Thus, they began to understand how a game playing experience depends not only on the particular game played, but also on how the game is approached.

Writing GameLogs helps highlight the tension between playing games "for fun" and for deeper understanding and analysis. Frank notes that "I don't believe it made me play the game any better than I normally would have." Playing a game with an eye for analysis requires a different approach. This surprised some students like George who commented that the assignment "took away from the experience of playing the game. It was like reading a really good book and stopping and taking notes. It's just not the same as reading it for pleasure all the way through with no interruption." Harrison even felt that games like *Grand Theft Auto* are "meant to be played and enjoyed, not to be thought out or analyzed." When faced with an assignment that required using their experience as a resource for analysis and understanding, students begin to wrestle with the notion that games are more than "consumer media goods" and can be engaged as cultural artifacts with embedded meaning and ideas. In this way, they can begin to approach, play, and understand videogames differently and thus become better prepared to study and learn about them.

> *"I came to analyze the way that I was playing, the way that I was actually using the games, and my experiences doing that. You never really think about that. I guess most people don't really think about what they're doing when they're playing games or how they're playing the games"* – **Isabel**

Expression and Collaboration

Students described writing GameLogs as a positive learning experience because it allows them to articulate ideas they have difficulty communicating, express themselves, share opinions and, to a lesser degree, collaborate in creating a shared understanding of a game. Patricia describes, "I thought I knew the characters, but trying to explain their personalities and habits was quite hard until I really sat down and did the GameLog." For Orianna, writing a GameLog provided a different opportunity:

> *"It was interesting to see whether other people thought the same things about the game that I did. I was playing an abstract game and was curious to see if they had the same notion of it as I did. Or, was I completely off-base? It was hard for me to know what should be interpreted and what not. And so, it helped to read what other people think."* – **Orianna**

In both classes studied, students were asked to write about their experience with a game from a relatively small list. Since GameLogs are publicly readable, this meant that students enjoyed access to the wealth of opinions, thoughts and experiences of their peers regarding the games they were playing and studying. As mentioned by Orianna, this allows students additional opportunities for reflection, as they read each others' GameLogs. Oriana's comment also shows her reflections on how other people experience the game she played. In this way, she moves away from one of the aspects of a naïve understanding of videogames I described in Chapter 4. I should note that the students were not explicitly asked to read each others' work, but most chose to do so anyway. By reading their peer's thoughts and reflections, students began to understand how different people experience games differently (moving away from a naïve understanding of games), saw what their peers chose to focus on, and learned about aspects of a game that they may not have noticed or cared to think about. This experience can help deepen one's understanding of games. It also helps students consider the reasons and motives people might have for playing games they may not care for.

> *"I've never understood why people play The Sims. So here I was playing it and trying to get into those reasons. And so, it was interesting to read other people's thoughts and then think about it, because I didn't feel the game that way. What actually grabbed them was something that I didn't care for, but now I had a sense of what it was. To me, that was totally unexpected."* – **Quentin**

Some students also took advantage of the feature on the site that allowed them to comment on each other's GameLog entries. Comments posted were generally supportive and friendly. There were no incidents of deviant behavior such as personal attacks or inappropriate comments. This could be explained by the prior knowledge students had of each other. Raphael's comment highlights how an appreciative audience can positively affect the experience of writing and reflecting:

> *"I liked the feedback. It made me feel less worried that I was a horrible video game player and concentrate more on my experience. I don't necessarily want tips on how to play the game but commenting on my blog makes the blog experience better. Why have a blog in the first place if nobody else is going to read it?"* - **Raphael**

Some students, aware that they were going to write about their experience and that this would be read by others, chose to change the way they played the game in order to communicate or demonstrate something to the potential readers.

Jackson describes, "Generally I just play a game for a quick 30 minutes and then I can then get up and leave. But this time, I know it's going to happen beforehand [referring to playing *The Sims*], so I'm thinking how can I play it so I can write about it and share the experience rather than just sitting with the *The Sims* and just doing just random things for an hour or so."

The quality of the student writing was another issue raised during the course of our study. Students perceived writing in a blog as less formal and more relaxed than a traditional class writing assignment. Their entries were commonly riddled with grammatical and orthographical errors considered inappropriate for a formal assignment (for a review of similar issues of quality in journalistic blogs see Seipp, 2002).

However, the informality was perceived by the students as liberating. In taking a more relaxed approach, students reported they could express themselves more freely and were able to come up with insights more readily. Heather describes, "if [the instructor] had told us to play these games and write an essay about our experience, I wouldn't have seen the way that I played the game, the way that I wrote about it in the journals. My journal logs are more personal. I cheated! [in the game] I wouldn't have written about that in an essay. I wouldn't have talked about my experiences in the same way, in the same fashion." Since their writing occurred closer to the actual experience, they could capture information, impressions, insight, and feelings that were more personal and concrete.

The course instructor also perceived the value in this different kind of assignment as he noted that "maybe this is something I should change. Part of this is because my courses were focused on this end result. I have this sort of old-school insistence on synthetic research output – a term paper. Maybe it's not always the best demonstration of a particular kind of mastery. Maybe if I taught the undergrads again I would have them write a bunch of little things, and that would be the right answer."

In the same way that the field notes of a researcher's observations are the initial step in the process of writing an academic research paper, a students' GameLog entries help lay the foundations on which learning and understanding can happen.

Facilitating Deeper Understanding

In addition to changing the way they related to videogames as a medium, students reported that the reflective writing activity helped them achieve a deeper understanding of the games they were studying. "It helped me understand a bit more. When you play through, you're kind of in it, so it's hard to have an insight. Writing afterward is like looking in from the outside. It helps you put on a different perspective" says Jeremy. Like many of his classmates, writing on multiple occasions about different sessions of gameplay helped him understand a particular game in different ways and focus on specific elements or aspects of a game that would previously have gone unnoticed.

Kathy describes her experience with Façade, an interactive drama game, where the player witnesses, and tries to mediate, the marital crisis of the non-player characters Trip and Grace:

"I begin connecting any little action I executed in the game to any response that the interacting characters gave. For example, two of the three times I played, Trip recounted several things I had said throughout the evening, and I begin to connect that somehow

he thought I said such-and-such when I had actually meant something totally different. Looking back over the conversation as I was journaling, I began to realize how the characters interpreted different comments depending on their mood at the moment. For example, when Grace was angry because of a previous comment by Trip, she always interpreted my comments as invading on the territory of the marriage." – **Kathy**

There is also evidence supporting the idea that students engaging with the four contexts of understanding games[11] I defined in Chapter 3. Isabel describes: "I began to realize that you can't describe a game like a movie. Well, except for the pre-game movie-like clip [referring to cut scenes[12]]. In describing a game, you have to get into different details than movies, even though when you look at someone playing a game, they can look very similar." Isabel's reflection shows her contextualizing games with respect to other cultural forms, in this case movies (1rst context).

Similarly, Neil begins to understand the relationship that a game such as *The Sims* has with virtual pets like *Tamagotchi*. He has realized that the core gameplay of both games is the same, and that both rely on a particular human motivation (to nurture). In this sense, he is understanding aspects of *The Sims* in context with other games (2nd context). Neil describes:

"The characters in The Sims reminded me of Tamagotchi pets. The Sims' characters had the same addictive feeling of caring as the Tamagotchi pets. My thought while playing was that the characters were more like children, or a pet, the player has to take care of. The user has to feed them, make them shower, and do other basic human functions. When it gets down to the bare requirements that a Sims character needs for fulfillment, they are the same needs that a pet dog would have." - **Neil**

Orianna's experience is similar to Neil's as she begins to explore the similarities and differences between two games that are part of *The Legend of Zelda* series (2nd context). Additionally, she also wonders about the role that different generations of hardware play in shaping the experience of playing each game (3rd context).

"I played Zelda [Wind Waker] and writing about it made me think about its gameplay in comparison to other games I had

---

[11] 1rst context: games in culture, 2nd context: games and other games, 3rd context: games and technology, 4th context: deconstruction and components.
[12] A cut scene is a brief, generally non-interactive interlude in a game. It is usually used to advance a game's plot.

played. I hadn't really played Zelda since the NES. It was really interesting for me to think about the one I was playing on the Gamecube, compared to the original NES version, because they are two completely different types of game now. The hardware systems are totally different, what you can do is totally different, and so on. However, it was still strangely familiar..." **– Orianna**

Harrison commented on the fact that "when you analyze the game you can't help but notice the many shortcomings in the game. [These issues] can be easily ignored if you're just playing, but when you write about it you can't help but think about it." Harrison's comment illustrates another issue the students are beginning to come to terms with: distinguishing the "parts" of a game and how they function, from the impact they have on the game and the experience of playing it, as a whole (4th context for understanding games). Jeremy illustrates, "I noticed that looking in from the outside, the game maybe is pretty simple and even flawed, but when I played it, the game was much better. It was like understanding how the whole was greater than each of its parts."

By reflecting on their game playing activity, students like Dominic note, "I was able to see that there were more things to the game then just following the missions." The reflective process helps them realize certain non-obvious insights as they begin to identify components of games and see how they interact and create certain experiences. For example, Meredith noticed that feedback from non-player characters serves as a reward in *Harvest Moon*, while Louis had an insight on the effect that the character creation system has on the narrative in games like *Oblivion* and *Knights of the Old Republic*. Nigel debated how the voice of Carl, the player-controlled character in *Grand Theft Auto: San Andreas*, helped create a less immersive experience than that of *Grand Theft Auto III*, despite the similarities in their gameplay. In addition to understanding games from the 4th context, Nigel and Louis reveal they are also considering the 2nd context for understanding games. Even students like Jessica, who felt that the GameLogging experience detracted from her enjoyment of the game, remarked, "I did understand the game more than I did before." By writing their GameLogs, students begin to understand the role that certain elements play in the experience or design of a game. They can also begin to relate them to each other, and see how sometimes the same elements appear in other games, playing different roles.

Understanding a particular game, however, can mean more than the ability to deconstruct it, or view it holistically. Maurice describes that writing a GameLog "helps me get in tune with what I just did and keep track of what's going on over the long term. Journaling gets me to think of the game outside of playing the game itself." Maurice begins to make sense of his experience and can understand the game in a broader context. Orianna summarized the role of the experience as helping to "start thinking about more than just the gameplay, but also the physical aspects of sitting down and playing a game, analyzing them culturally, and how do they relate to other practices. How do games relate to our experiences, not just with games, but with other people and the world, how have they changed? It's about trying to think about games as a much broader subject." I found that the experience of writing about their gameplay experience was useful for the students in helping them achieve a deeper understanding of videogames.

Shifting Modes of Play

In Chapter 4, I reported how game studies class instructors often found that students had difficulties in stepping back from their role as "gamers" or "fans". One of the particular challenges students in these classes face is that of confusing playing games for fun and entertainment with playing them for critical analysis. While I did not study, or observe, students playing games, I did find evidence that students began to play and approach games differently due to their experience with GameLog. For example, Nate describes how he began paying more attention to details because "keeping a GameLog forced me to come up with content to write about, and the only way to bring forth quality content was to examine the game through a critical eye and notice all of the extra details." In another example, Jarrod, in the context of his experience with *Grand Theft Auto III*, reflects his interactions with characters in the game. He notices how his insights come from the fact that he was playing the game differently.

> *"This was a very interesting experience, because when you play a game like Grand theft auto, you don't really think about how the players are interacting, you just play. It was neat to really think about why it was necessary for the characters to interact the way they did, and it really makes you think about how limited certain possibilities for interaction really are. Yet at the same time you can see that there are still a ton of other ways to interact with the characters."* - **Jarrod**

Jarrod's impressions are mirrored by Zoey, who describes some of the ways that writing a GameLog can influence how games are played.

> *"Depending on the gamer and the game, the idea of game logs can influence the playing of a game. By using such a log, gamers can keep track of what has happened in their game. They can help decide on new strategies that would not otherwise be thought of.*

Also, it helps to keep track of what the gamer has tried or would like to try in the game. In addition, the player may get new ideas from just writing one." **- Zoey**

So, in what ways can blogging about gameplay experiences support the process of shifting modes of play? Summarizing, students found that blogging about their gameplay experiences changed the way they played games. In particular, they began:

- Paying greater attention to details
    - Notice things that would otherwise have gone undetected
- Planning ahead
    - Keep track of what they would like to try in a game
- Playing games with broader issues or questions in mind
- Trying out new actions and in-game activities

Log Entry Analysis

In the last section, I discussed the students' perceptions and feelings about writing a reflective online journal of their gameplay experience. I also showed how they begin to demonstrate a deeper understanding of videogames. The experience of writing a blog of gameplay experiences also supported students in playing games differently. Now I will describe the results of my analysis of students' GameLog entries.

A total of 137 entries were written by 35 students (24 U-class, 11 G-class). The average entry was 235 words long with a standard deviation of 119 words. The shortest entry was only 17 words long, while the longest was 773 words. Similarly to my analysis of the interviews I reported earlier, the student's GameLog entries were analyzed and coded in an iterative process to identify and refine theoretical categories, propositions, and conclusions as they emerged from the data (Glaser and Strauss, 1967). In this case, however, I was interested in getting a sense of the kinds of things students wrote about and how they wrote them. Would they tell the story of what happened when they played the game, or would they write about their difficulties playing? Would they approach the assignment as a chance to analyze specific aspects or would they try to convince the reader on the merits (or lack thereof) of the game played? In particular, my analysis would hopefully show evidence of reflective gameplay, identify common patterns across student entries, and help explain why those patterns exist and what role they played in students' understanding of games. The process used was similar to that of the interview analysis described earlier in terms of the iterative coding (refer to sub-section titled Student Impressions on page 87).

From my analysis, I was able to identify common patterns across entries. From these patterns, I determined six prototypical styles of GameLog entry: overview, narrative, comparative analysis, plan/ hypothesis, investigation, and insight/analysis (see Table 6). The diversity of styles found illustrates the multiplicity of ways students approached the task of reflecting on their gameplay experiences. Not all the students approached the task in the same way, and students often changed their approach from one GameLog entry to another. Also, some students wrote entries that took multiple approaches and mixed styles in the same entry. This was common in longer entries.

Table 6: GameLog entry styles

Style	Brief Definition
Overview	General description of the game.
Narrative	Description of what the player did and what happened during the game session.
Comparative Analysis	Description and comparison of specific elements of a game with another game.
Plan/Hypothesis	Description of goals or questions the player wants answered followed by a plan for achieving them.
Investigation	Description of an investigation or experiment performed during the gameplay session.
Insight/Analysis	Description of a specific insight or analysis of an element or aspect of the game.

Table 7 shows the distribution of the frequency of different styles used by the students in each of the classes. For example, by the end of the assignment, 41.7% of the students in the U-Class had written using three different styles.[13] The frequencies are divided by class type because students in the U-Class wrote fewer entries (avg. of 3.1 entries per student) than those in the G-Class (avg. of 5.4 entries per student). Recall that the assignment for each class differed in the number of games students were

---

[13] Not all of the students who used three styles wrote using the same combination of styles. So, one student might have written an overview, narrative and an investigation while another might have written an overview, narrative and comparative analysis.

asked to play and write about (one or three games). Despite the differences in the number of entries written, Table 7 shows that there are no significant differences in the variety of styles used by the students in each class. This table also shows that most students did not strongly favor one style with only 8.6% of the students in both classes using only one style for all their entries.

Table 7: Distribution of frequency of styles used by participants

Number of Styles Used	U-Class	G-Class	Combined
1	8.3%	9.1%	8.6%
2	16.7%	18.2%	17%
3	41.7%	18.2%	34.3%
4	25%	36.3%	28.6%
5	8.3%	9.1%	8.6%
6	0%	9.1%	2.9%

I will now describe each style, show excerpts from GameLog entries that exemplify the style described, and also discuss the pedagogical role that each of these styles can play as students are learning and creating a deeper understanding of games. The excerpts are reproduced verbatim from the students' GameLogs. For reasons of privacy, the usernames the students used to write have been replaced with pseudonyms.

Overview

The Overview style consists of a general description of the game written for a reader who is assumed to be unfamiliar with the game in question. Entries written in this style generally attempt to provide some sort of context about the game being played. For example, it may refer to earlier games in a series or other games that may be similar. Additionally, there might be some reference to the circumstances that illustrate why author decided to play the particular game or if there is any prior history with the game in question. Entries written in the Overview style are also often accompanied by criticism or praise for certain aspects of the game.

In the following example, Zach describes how *Boundish* is part of a broader series of games. Although Zach's overview does not provide much in the way of detail, it is interesting to note that he presents *Boundish* as a tribute to early videogames, placing it in the context of other games (2nd context of understanding games).

> *"Boundish is part of Nintendo's Bit Generation series. The complete series includes Soundvoyager, Orbital, Coloris, Boundish, Digidrive, Dotstream, and Dialhex. I just ordered the complete series from eBay, and I can't wait for them to arrive.*
>
> *Of the five games on the cart, I've spent most of my time tonight playing Box Juggling and Human League. Both of these games are best described as Pong variants and tributes to early moments in videogames."* **- Zach** (Boundish)

Emily begins her first entry for John Conway's Life by describing the rules under which it operates.

> *"To begin with, here are the "rules" of the game:*
> *For a space that is 'populated': Each cell with one or no neighbors dies, as if by loneliness. Each cell with four or more neighbors dies, as if by overpopulation. Each cell with two or three neighbors survives. For a space that is 'empty' or 'unpopulated' Each cell with three neighbors becomes populated[...]"* – **Emily (John Conway's Life)**

Writing an Overview requires that the student reflect on the game and consider how it should be presented to someone who isn't necessarily familiar with it. It is an exercise in contextualizing the game for an uninformed reader.

Writing an Overview requires dealing with questions like: What are the important features? What is the core gameplay? What does the reader need to know in order to get a feeling for what this game is like? Additionally, it can be an exercise in reflecting on prior experience and knowledge of the game in question. For example, students might have to recollect what they've heard about a particular game or reflect on what their pre-conceived notions of the game might be. What kind of experience do they think they will have? How will their experience account for what they have heard about this game? In the case of writing about games they might have played previously, students are also prompted to recall their prior experiences. Did they enjoy the game? For what reasons? How do they think this new experience might differ? What memories does this game bring back? 63% of the participants wrote at least one entry that was an Overview and 21% of the entries were written in this style. Additionally, 75% of the entries written as an Overview were the initial (earliest) entry written for a game.

Narrative

An entry written in the Narrative style consists of a description, generally written in first person, of what the player did, and what happened during the game session. It is usually accompanied by descriptions of relevant or necessary parts of the game and is interspersed with minor insights and observations made by the player.

Samuel describes his goals and impressions of *Grand Theft Auto III* while describing the activities he has engaged with in the game.

> *"After that, I decided to do Joey's last mission as well: The Getaway. This mission was ridiculously easy compared to his previous one. I had to be the driver for a bank robbery. After the robbery, I had three stars, but immediately dropped one by picking up a police bribe in an alley. I then drove to a Pay 'n Spray to get rid of the remaining two."* – **Samuel** (*Grand Theft Auto III*)

In this example Susan describes her interactions with some of the characters in Animal Crossing. She is starting to figure out how she could learn more about the other characters in the game but hasn't decided yet to investigate whether or not her notion is correct or not.

Through her entry, Susan is beginning to consider how characters "work" in Animal Crossing. In this way, she begins to understand this game in the context of its components and how they interact (4th context for understanding games).

> *"[...]The past couple of days I have been pestering Sable, the girl at the sewing machine. She just gets pissy and tells me to ask the clerk for help or tells me that she is very busy. Today, Derwin, one of my townsfolk, asked me to take a personality quiz. After answering a couple of questions, it told me that I was most like Pelly, the lovable pelican at the town center post office. Derwin went on to tell me more about Pelly's trustworthy attitude and personality. I guess if I answered the quiz differently I could learn*

about the personality of other characters." – **Susan** (Animal Crossing)

The Narrative style is well suited for describing general gameplay. When students write in this style, they revisit their experience and can begin to understand the relationships between their actions in the game, and the results, or effects, of those actions.

By recounting the events of their gameplay session, students can also begin to formulate questions and ideas that might be the focus of attention in later gameplay sessions. This style of entry was the most common with 42% of the entries belonging to this style. Also, 69% of the participants wrote at least one entry in this style.

Comparative Analysis

Entries written in the style of a Comparative Analysis describe specific elements of a game and compare them with a similar game, usually another game in a series. The comparative analysis usually includes recommendations to the reader or opinions regarding the differences noted. This style of entry often the result of reflecting on the 2nd context of understanding games, that of other games.

Richard comments on the differences in tone and humor between *Grand Theft Auto 2* and *Grand Theft Auto III (GTAIII)*.

He finds that although the general gameplay remains unchanged in both games, the integration of presentation and gameplay doesn't quite work as well in GTAIII as it does in its prequel.

> *"I was and still am a big fan of Grand Theft Auto 2. And here is where the problem arises for me, every time I play any of its successors I find traces of the old game lurking beneath each element that they tout. I feel that if one were to write down the formal rules of both the games down on paper, they wouldn't be significantly different. However, the execution of the latter games ruined something for me. GTA2 had a very tongue-in-cheek and comical approach to its presentation, the mob bosses jabbered in nonsensical tongue, the voiceovers were hilarious, even some of the missions had a wry sense of humour about them. All of which made the actual gameplay (essentially killing people) seem somewhat dissonant and eerily syncopated.*

> *GTA3 has these activities more or less as a matter of fact, and it takes a bit of fun out of it. I'm not a big fan of realism."*
> – **Richard** (Grand Theft Auto III)

Occasionally, entries in the comparative analysis style compare a game with the conventions of certain game genres such as role playing games (2nd context for understanding games). When playing *The Sims,* Mark notes how the process for designing characters might mirror that of role-playing games such as the paper and pencil game Dungeons & Dragons (D&D).

> *"The first thing I noticed in the create character screen was that the personality selector was similar to RPGs in the sense that you are given a set amount of resources to allot to certain kinds of traits such as niceness, playfulness, etc. Could these traits match up to D&D's abilities? Outgoing = Charisma. Active = Dexterity. Not much else works. Oh well. If only it mapped up one to one, then we could have your typical Sims player rolling d10s for Niceness and so forth."* – **Mark** (The Sims)

When writing a Comparative Analysis, students focus their attention on the differences and similarities between two games. They can begin to develop a deeper understanding of games by identifying elements common to both games, exploring how these elements play different roles in games, and how the resulting game experience may be similar or different (thus, supporting the 4th context of understanding games). Comparative Analysis style entries were usually written by students who had extensive prior experience with games that were related to the one being written about. This style of entry was also the least common accounting for only 11% of the entries. However, 31% of the students wrote at least one entry in this style.

Plan/Hypothesis

Entries in the Plan/Hypothesis style consist of a description of goals the player wants to achieve in the game or questions the player wants answered regarding the game. This is followed by a plan or strategy for achieving them. The plan is often accompanied by hypotheses about how the game works. The results of the plan are usually referred to in later entries.

In the following example, Cynthia outlines some of the things she would like to find out about *The Sims 2*. She also describes how she plans to set herself up in the game in order to explore the questions she has. Many of Cynthia's questions have to do with understanding how the game works, her questions begin to get at issues of understanding parts of games and how they interact (4th context for understanding games).

"I decided to start a new family. I chose a pre-made brother and sister to run a much more hands-off business. Now this is the coolest thing ever. Basically what I'm going to do is buy neat stuff and make other sims pay just to come onto my lot. Sweet! (I'm still planning to start off with a little extra money, this way I can figure things out. It's rough when they're uber poor and you don't even know what you're trying to do.)

Some things I'm curious to find out:

1) Will I be able to make enough money for them to survive? (naturally)

2) Can the business still grow when I'm not actually trying to sell things?

3) Can the business stay open when they're both at work?"
- Cynthia (*The Sims 2*)

Cynthia's example, above, also describes how she intends to "cheat" and start the game with more resources than she would generally be allowed[14]. In this way Cynthia describes how some students deal with some of the challenges posed by the medium of videogames described in Chapter 4. In the case of *The Sims 2*, Cynthia used a special code that allowed her characters to receive extra cash, thus enabling her to be in a position in the game where she could experiment and try things out without the fear of losing. By the end of the assignment, her understanding of how the game "works" had increased as she described: "I think I'm ready to start a new game now. I want to start from the beginning, no cheating."

In another example, Dominic describes some of the issues he has had with *Façade*. Dominic's entry shows him wrestling with some of the characteristics of a naïve understanding of games (see Chapter 4). He expresses a certain degree of frustration by his perceived lack of agency controlling the direction of the conversation he has with the other characters in the game (dealing with being successful at playing the game). He wonders whether or not this has to do with the way he is approaching the experience (as a game, rather than a real situation) and hopes that with further practice he will be able to "get the hang of it".

"I still don't feel like I really know how to communicate with the two. There is the obvious "hello," "how are you doing?" stuff that has minimal impact, but I don't seem to get any further. The two begin yelling at each other and all I can do is take sides with my responses. I don't really feel that I grasp the range of responses that are available to me. I am thinking of this like a game, and I think

---

[14] Cynthia refers to this explicitly in later entries.

they want me to think of it as a real situation and try what I would in real life. I am having problems transitioning to that way of thinking, maybe next time I will get the hang of it and start controlling to conversation more." – **Dominic** (Façade)

Thinking ahead, and formulating questions and hypothesis are important for fostering learning and understanding (Bransford et al., 2000). By writing a Plan/Hypothesis, a student can reflect on his understanding of a game, and come up with a way to correct or improve it. Entries written as Plan/Hypothesis were often followed by entries written in the style of an Investigation. This style of entry was used in 23% of the entries written. Also, 57% of the students wrote at least one entry in this style.

Investigation

Entries written in the style of an Investigation consist of a description of an investigation or experiment performed during the gameplay session. The objective, or reason, for the investigation is described followed by how the goal was pursued. What actually happened, together with insight that resulted from the investigation, is also recounted. Evidence for the insight usually comes from the results of the investigation itself.

In the following example, Thomas describes his interest in understanding how the player controlled character, an African American young man called CJ, is characterized in the game *Grand Theft Auto: San Andreas*. The game is set in late 1992 in the fictional state of San Andreas, which is based on sections of California and Nevada.

Thomas' example shows how students did not limit themselves to investigating aspects of gameplay or functionality, but also chose to explore other issues, such as representation and characterization. Although he doesn't mention it in the entry, in a follow-up interview Thomas described his interest in comparing the representation of characters in this game with that of hood films set in a similar timeline[15]. In this way, Thomas was seeking to better understand this game by contextualizing it with respect to a particular film genre (1st context for games understanding).

"I didn't want to simply run around the world, completely defining the main character, CJ. I wanted to catch a glimpse of a few cutscenes to see how the developer's characterize CJ. In order to get this done, I have to attempt a few missions. Not

---

[15]   Hood films are a genre which features aspects of primarily African American urban culture including street gangs, racial discrimination, and the problems of young black men coming of age. Two prototypical films of this genre are Menace II Society (1993), directed by Allen and Albert Hughes, and Boyz N the Hood (1991), directed by John Singleton.

only do these cutscenes develop the characters, but they advance the storyline. This particular mission has me picking up women for a rapper's party. When OG Loc, the rapper, is giving me my instructions he comes off as a lame, overly ambitious rapper with delusions of granduer. The whole time CJ is completely cool, understanding that Loc has less musical talent than Milli and Vanilli, but still playing along like he's the second coming of the Dr. Dre. In this cutscene we have humor, character development and a small suggestion that the player is somehow "cool". We see an imbecile like OG Loc and can relate to CJ's feeling of superiority."
– Thomas (*GTA: San Andreas*)

Charlotte describes how she, upon discovering additional modes of interaction in *Façade,* began to investigate what would happen in the game if she effectively ignored the game's primary mode of interaction: typing written text.

Note that by ensuring that her interactions, while non-textual, are appropriate to the situations in the game, she is not attempting to subvert, or break, the game. Rather, she is investigating the range of options available, and thus exploring the structural components of the game and how they interact (4th context for understanding games).

"For this time, I tried not saying anything the entire time. Instead, I found out that if you moved close enough to either of the characters, the cursor would change into one of three others. The others included the options to hug, comfort, or kiss the character in front of you. So, I changed my strategy slightly once again to see what the characters would do if I didn't say a word the entire time but I would hug, comfort, or kiss them depending on the situation and the previous comments and would pick up random objects in the room. Needless to say I got a lot of interesting comments..."
– Charlotte (Façade)

From a learning perspective, writing an Investigation is pedagogically similar to the Plan/Hypothesis. They both show that the student is actively engaging his knowledge and understanding of a game by formulating questions, planning courses of actions to resolve those questions.

The Investigation additionally describes students executing plans of actions and ultimately commenting on the results of those actions. This style of entry was used in 13% of the entries written and only 37% of the students wrote at least one entry in this style.

Insight/Analysis

The Insight/Analysis style of entry consists of a description of a specific insight that happened while playing, or an analysis of a specific element or aspect of the game. The analysis is usually accompanied by supporting evidence from the gameplay session. Occasionally, there is some commentary on the effects or meaning of the insight.

In the following example, Victor describes how he has come to realize that the design of the first playable area in *Legend of Zelda: Wind Waker* has been designed to implicitly introduce players to the basic skills they will need to play the rest of the game.

Many games have areas or sections labeled "tutorials" that are separate from the rest of the game. Victor notes how, for this game, the designers chose instead to carefully design the first area, Outset Island, to support their "explanation" of the game by ensuring that all of the relevant skills necessary for success in the game were covered (4th context of understanding games).

> "*Outset Island and its inhabitants exist less as people and more as a tutorial for novice players to learn the particular game-isms of The Legend of Zelda series. It's actually interesting to note the various ways the landscape of the island, the NPCs living there, and even the small sidetasks are all explicitly designed to acclimate players to the basic controller functions that will be necessary to play the rest of the game. The simplest concepts: the necessity to collect rupees to buy things (reinforced in multiple ways), the basic combat system, and even the item collection/buying/button assignment mechanics are all explained at this juncture.*"– **Victor** (*Legend of Zelda: Wind Waker*)

Timothy's entry describes some of the challenges of designing games that give players freedom to navigate large environments (often referred to as open-world games). He notes how *Okami's* open environments can sometimes be at odds with the objectives the player is tasked with completing, particularly when the player is unsure of where these objectives should be met. Like Victor's entry before, Timothy also shows the beginnings of an understanding of the components of games and how they interact (4th context for understanding games).

> "*One mission I encountered involved trying to rescue a boys dog. This mission was extremely frustrating because due to the open world nature it took me a long time to figure out where I was supposed to go. Eventually I ended up finding how to enter a cave*

*and completed a Zelda-like dungeon "level" to rescue the dog. [..]
This type of game-design is interesting to me. It creates discrete
"levels" but places them within an open world environement as
to simulate non-linearity. In reality the game is fairly linear, but
provides for a lot of exploration within the world. Often times
exploration is necessary for progression of the game. In trying to
find the dog I searched all the areas that I had previously explored
and came up empty until I finally found the correct cave. This
is an issue I believe open world games can cause. If direction
and focus is not clear then it may become difficult to locate
objectives. Sometimes it can just be frustrating to have to run all
over the game's world to find what you are looking for. Both of
these problems were present when I was trying to find the dog."*
– Timothy (Okami)

Students writing entries in the style of an Insight/Analysis are practicing analytical skills that are important for learning. Writing in this style can help a student explore aspects of a game in a deeper way than they may be used to. Additionally, especially when considering multiple entries for the same game, students can analyze different aspects of the same game.

This style of entry was used in 26% of the entries written. This style was also quite common with 63% of the students writing at least one entry in this style.

Discussion

My results show that the self-reported impressions that students have regarding the educational value of the GameLog assignment align with my analysis of what they wrote, and how they wrote, in their GameLog assignments.

In each case, I have shown how students begin to understand games more deeply. Also, each of the styles I found can play an important pedagogical role. For instance, the Plan/Hypothesis, Investigation, and Insight/Analysis styles are related to creating a deeper understanding of a particular game. The ability to pose questions, create a plan in order to achieve some understanding, execute the plan, and finally reflect on its results are important skills necessary for achieving a deep understanding of a subject matter (Edelson et al., 1999).

I reported that not all the students adopted all the prototype styles, though most students adopted different styles as they wrote their entries. It is an open question whether or not students should be provided with further guidance on how they should write their GameLog entries. Should certain styles be favored over others? Can I assume that students are prepared to write in all the styles I've observed?

Course instructors might want to scaffold students adopting certain styles based on their particular learning goals. For example, courses with a strong emphasis on player experience, might want to encourage the narrative style while a course on game history might prefer comparative analyses.

It is also an open question how useful was each style for each student. Were some styles better suited to certain students? Were other styles, for example Narrative and Overview, used as "fallbacks" for students that didn't feel like they knew what to write about or didn't have anything particular to say? It would also be interesting to see whether or not there are tendencies towards more reflective styles of entries as understanding and experience with the game increases.

Currently, there are hints of this as 62% of the students final entries for a particular game were in a more reflective style (Plan/Hypothesis, Investigation, or Insight/Analysis). However, further investigation is required.

The structure of the assignment also played an important role in allowing, and also guiding, students in writing about their experience. Students were asked to write three entries, each on a different gameplay session, about the same game. This kind of assignment is unusual in traditional learning environments where students aren't expected to re-visit and write about the same thing multiple times.

Students whose first GameLog entry was written in the Overview style found that they had to write something different for their latter entries. This guided them into focusing their gameplay sessions so that they could analyze and write about specific issues, compare aspects of the game with other games, or start posing questions they could investigate in future gameplay sessions. In other words, they began to plan ahead and think about what they wanted to explore or understand in future game sessions in order to have something to write about. This also helped them begin to approach the way they play a game differently. Instead of focusing on "just" having fun, they opted to train their eye on specific aspects or devised plans and experiments to test their ideas. The structure of the assignment was thus important in promoting skills and practices that are important for seriously understanding games.

In traditional learning environments, students get only one chance to "get it right", after that they move on to the next assignment. Writing on multiple occasions about the same game helps incorporate iterative practices that have shown useful positive learning benefits in other contexts, such as science learning (Kolodner et al., 1998).

As described earlier, the quality of the student writing was another issue raised during the course of our study. The instructor noted how perhaps his emphasis on the term paper as a means of demonstrating expertise might be misplaced. However, the broader issue might not lie in the requirement for the term paper per se. Rather, the issue lies in asking whether or not the students are prepared, and have the skills to adequately synthesize their knowledge and understanding in the form of a formal written argument (the term paper). Although the students' entries were, generally speaking, poorly written in terms of grammar and orthography, they were undoubtedly valuable from the perspective of practicing the kinds of analytical and synthetic skills they will require later. As I noted earlier, in the same way that the field notes of a researcher's observations are the initial step in the process of writing an academic research paper, a students' GameLog entries help lay the foundations on which learning and understanding can happen.

One of my goals for this chapter was to explore the 3rd question I posed: (Q3) How can we help students leverage knowledge from personal experiences with games to create abstract and deeper knowledge? In this chapter I have shown how blogging can be used to support reflective gameplay and thus, a deeper understanding of games. I have also shown how it can help students begin to learn to modes of gameplay, in particular shifting from playing "for fun", towards an inquiry of gameplay that can be useful for insight or analysis.

In the following chapter I will explore this same question from a different perspective: How can participating in the Game Ontology Project help students use their personal experiences and knowledge of videogames to make connections with abstract concepts and ideas while contributing meaningfully and legitimately to the academic study of games?

88

CHAPTER 6: UNDERSTANDING GAMES WHILE CONTRIBUTING TO GAME STUDIES

In this chapter I explore the same question as in the last chapter: (Q3) How can we help students leverage knowledge from personal experiences with games to create abstract and deeper knowledge? However, I explore another way to answer this question: How can participating in the Game Ontology Project help students use their personal experiences and knowledge of videogames to make connections with abstract concepts and ideas while contributing meaningfully and legitimately to the academic study of games? As I explore this question, I will also seek to find an answer to another of the questions I posed in Chapter 1: (Q4) What role can novices play in a professional knowledge-building community of practice?

First, I will outline some of the educational research that informs how I explore these questions. Then, I will describe the Game Ontology Project (GOP), a wiki-enabled hierarchy of elements of gameplay used by game studies researchers. In principle, as suggested by literature on communities of practice and knowledge building, participating in the GOP can help students use their personal experiences and knowledge to make connections with the abstract concepts and notions in the ontology. Since the ontology is actively used by game studies researchers, it also provides an opportunity for learners to participate and contribute meaningfully and authentically. However, how can we make the GOP approachable and useful to students? Also, how can we evaluate whether or not the students' participation was legitimate? I then describe how the GOP was used in a university-level games class. The results of this experience show that it helped students reflect on their prior experience with videogames and that they used this to gain a deeper understanding of videogames. In order to answer the question of whether or not the students' participation was legitimate, my analysis also includes an evaluation by game studies experts on the quality, type, and role played by the students' contributions. Finally, the results of this experience, both positive and negative, will frame a discussion of unsolved issues and future implications.

Authenticity for Learning and Participation as Learning

Learning research has argued the importance of providing students with an authentic context for fostering learning (Shaffer and Resnick, 1999). For example, project-based inquiry science (Blumenfeld et al., 1991), has focused on ensuring that what students do in the classroom somehow reflects or recreates some aspect of the real world outside of the learning environment. Others help learners interact with subject matter experts or non-school members who can serve as mentors, share knowledge, or answer questions (Songer, 1996; O'Neill and Gomez, 1998; Ellis and Bruckman, 2002). It has also been argued that using the tools and methods of a discipline encourages learning in that community of practice (Lave and Wenger, 1991). For example, students might learn history by "making history" as professional historians do (Kobrin et al., 1993) or engage with mathematical problems as mathematicians (D'Ambrosio, 1995). However, most learning in traditional environments is disconnected from external communities of practice and disciplines. For example, students might design and carry out scientific experiments that, while valuable pedagogically, do not contribute to science itself. Allowing students to meaningfully participate in authentic practices that contribute to a larger body of knowledge is difficult for a variety of reasons. For instance, real-world science is often not accessible to students because authentic activities that are interesting to students are too open-ended and require content knowledge and scientific thinking that students do not have the supports to realize (Edelson, 1998).

If we understand learning as a process of transformation of participation (Rogoff, 1994), of both absorbing and being absorbed in a "culture of practice", the lack of meaningful connections between novices (students) and larger communities of practice (experts, scientists, etc.) can be problematic. Lave and Wenger (1991) describe how learning occurs through legitimate peripheral participation (LPP). LPP describes how novice members of a community often begin participating in peripheral tasks that contribute to the goals of the community. These activities, while typically simple, are valued and important to the community as a whole (Lave and Wenger, 1991). Thus, how we can design learning environments that: 1) are approachable to learners, 2) allow learners to contribute legitimately to external communities of practice, 3) support visibility and access to the practices of a broader community?

Game Ontology Project

The challenges faced by students with respect to a lack of critical vocabulary for talking about games are perhaps unsurprising due to the newness of game studies as described in Chapter 2. Many game designers and professionals, noting the lack of a unified vocabulary for describing existing games and thinking through the design of new ones, have called for a design language for games (Costikyan, 1994; Church, 1999; Kreimeier, 2002). These calls have been answered in multiple ways. For instance, many of the proposed approaches focus on offering aid to the designer, either in the form of design patterns (Kreimeier, 2002; Björk and Holopainen, 2005), which name and describe design elements, or in the closely-related notion of design rules, which offer advice and guidelines for specific design situations (Fabricatore et al., 2002; Falstein, 2004). Each of these approaches are constantly evolving, growing, and adapting to the ever-changing landscape of videogames. The ever-growing size of collections of gameplay design patterns, design rules, or terminology can be daunting to students who can easily feel overwhelmed and not know from where to start.

The Game Ontology Project (GOP) is another approach. The GOP is developing a game ontology that identifies the important structural elements of games and the relationships between them, organizing them hierarchically (Zagal et al., 2007). The term ontology is borrowed from computer science, and it refers to the identification and (oftentimes formal) description of entities within a domain. In describing structural elements of games, the ontology's entries are often derived from common game terminology (e.g. level and score) and are then refined by both abstracting more general concepts and by identifying more precise or specific concepts.

Each ontology entry consists of a title or name, a description of the element, examples of games that embody the element, a parent element, potentially one or more child elements, and potentially one or more part elements (elements related by the part-of relation). The examples describe how the element is instantiated in specific games. There are two types of examples, strong and weak. Strong examples are "obvious" or canonical exemplars of a particular entry, while weak examples describe borderline cases of games that partially reify the element. Table 8 shows an example of a particular ontology entry called "To Own".

The GOP is distinct from design rule and design pattern approaches that offer imperative advice to designers (Fabricatore et al., 2002; Falstein, 2004). The project does not have as one of its goals to describe rules for creating good games, but rather to identify the abstract commonalities and differences in design elements across a wide range of concrete examples. The ontological approach is also distinct from genre analyses and related attempts to answer the question "what is a game?" Rather than develop definitions to distinguish between games/non-games or among different types of games (Elverdam and Aarseth, 2007), the GOP focuses on analyzing of design elements that cut across a wide range of games. The GOP does not attempt to classify games according to their characteristics and/or mechanics (Lundgren and Björk, 2003), but to describe the design space of games.

Table 8: Example Ontology entry - "To Own"

Name	To Own
Parent	Entity Manipulation
Children	To Capture, To Possess, To Exchange
Description	Entities can own other game entities. Ownership does not carry any inherent meaning, other than the fact that one entity is tied to another. Changes in ownership can not be initiated by the owned entity. Ownership can change the attributes or abilities of either the owned or owning entity. Ownership can be used to measure performance, either positive or negative. Ownership is never permanent; the possibility of losing ownership separates ownership from an inherent attribute or ability of an entity. Ownership of an entity can change in variety of ways, including voluntary and involuntary changes of ownership. It is important to note the difference between owning an entity, and using an entity. For example, in *Super Mario Bros,* when Mario collides with a mushroom, the mushroom is immediately used and removed from the game world. Mario never owns the mushroom.
Strong Example	In *Super Mario World*, Mario can collect mushrooms (or fire flowers or feathers) to use later. Mario owns these entities and can choose when to use them.
Weak Example	In *Ico*, the player character must protect a girl called Yorda. While the player only directly controls Ico, his actions are very closely tied to leading, guiding and protecting Yorda. One could argue that Ico, in effect, owns Yorda because of the way they are tied to each other.

The GOP also distinguishes itself from other approaches by using prototype theory as an alternative to traditional classification. Traditionally, things are in the same category if and only if they all have the same properties in common. The GOP has found that for many concepts in games there is no such list of properties that supports a binary category membership function. Thus, many parts of the ontology have fuzzy boundaries regarding what games exemplify them (or have aspects that exemplify them). This is particularly evident in the GOP's use of examples. These examples are important because they help define the center of the category, and illustrate the nuances and interpretations an ontological definition may have.

Finally, the GOP is also different from other approaches due to its hierarchical nature and its support for multiple levels of abstraction. While other approaches, such as Bjork and Holopainen's gameplay design patterns establish relationships and dependencies between patterns (Björk and Holopainen, 2005), these relationships are not hierarchical and generally occur at the same level of abstraction. In the case of the GOP, entries at the top are generally abstractions and generalizations of those entries beneath them in the hierarchy. Entries at the bottom are generally much more specific.

Affordances for Authentic Learning and Legitimate Participation

In principle, the Game Ontology Project, used in the context of a games class, provides students with opportunities to learn and acquire a critical vocabulary about games, participate in the creation of new knowledge about games, and also gain a deeper understanding of games. In particular, the structure and organization of the ontology, together with some affordances of the technology on which it resides, should be valuable for promoting learning.

Game Ontology Project Affordances

As described earlier, the GOP distinguishes itself from other approaches due to its reliance on strong and weak examples as well as its hierarchical approach. By relying on strong, or canonical, and weak or borderline examples, the GOP affords the exploration of the space of game design. Categorizations aren't binary, leaving ample room for discussion and revisitation. The ontology's reliance on examples also provides a clear entry point for students to legitimately and peripherally participate. Students could leverage their own personal knowledge by adding examples from games they are familiar while also refining those entries that already exist. Participating in this way, students could, in principle, begin to associate what they know about games with the knowledge created in the GOP and identify those things they may know implicitly.

The GOP's hierarchical structure accommodates varying levels of abstraction that can facilitate student understanding and navigation. Students may begin by exploring entries that are more concrete (at the bottom), and, as they become more comfortable with the definitions, they can climb the hierarchy exploring those that are more abstract. This provides a natural way to understand the broader context of certain entries. For example, students might begin by exploring an entry called "Level". By going "up" and reading about its parent entry, "Spatial Segmentation" they begin understanding that "Level" is a specific type of "Spatial Segmentation" and what role this plays in a game. The ontology also describes other types of segmentation that aren't spatial, and students have access to a framework that helps them understand how "Level" relates to a "cousin" entry called "Wave" (an entry under the "Segmentation of Gameplay" sub-hierarchy that isn't a child entry of "Spatial Segmentation").

The GOP affords knowledge building. Recall that knowledge building is a process by which ideas that are valuable to a community are continually produced and improved. The result of knowledge building is the creation and modification of public knowledge, knowledge that lives "in the world" and is available to be worked on and used by other people (Scardamalia and Bereiter, 2002). Scardamalia and Bereiter (1991) have taken this idea into the realm of formal learning by proposing knowledge building activities as a way of altering discourse patterns in the classroom so that students would assume what they called "higher levels of agency", i.e., come to see themselves as constructors of meaning.. The core elements of successful knowledge building are using ideas as objects to think with, viewing ideas as improvable, and fostering idea diversity. As learners better understand the problems and questions they are exploring, ideas change and improve. Knowledge building systems require a critical mass of articulated ideas before they become useful. The GOP provides an existing structure and content that serves to mitigate this challenge. The existing content thus can scaffold knowledge building by providing guidance about what entries (ideas) should look like, how they might be structured and organized, and how they might be refined over time.

Knowledge-building is driven by discourse (Scardamalia and Bereiter, 1994). In particular, knowledge building discourse focuses on problems and depths of understanding. For knowledge building, explaining is the major challenge. This is very similar to the raison d'être of the GOP: identifying, understanding, and describing structural elements of games. Knowledge building discourse is decentralized with a focus on collective knowledge. The knowledge of those who are more advanced does not circumscribe what is to be learned or investigated, and novices push discourse towards definition and clarification. In the case of games, not everyone is an expert in every game. Thus, there is room for everyone to provide their own examples and knowledge. Also, the non-static nature of the entries implies that anyone can provide examples that push discourse towards refining and clarifying entries. It is often the case in the GOP that when an entry has too many weak examples, its definition either needs to be refined or a new sub-entry needs to be created for which those weak examples become strong examples.

Knowledge building discourse should interact productively within more broadly conceived knowledge building communities. Students using the GOP have the opportunity to interact, contribute and participate directly in an on-going project that is active and used by game studies researchers. They have the chance to truly participate as knowledge builders in an existing community of practice. In summary, for students, the GOP facilitates:

1. Leveraging the use of personal knowledge of games
2. Browsing and learning by incorporating varying levels of abstraction
3. An environment focused on discourse where knowledge is continually refined and improved

Wiki-Related Affordances

The GOP currently resides on a wiki-enabled website. A wiki is a type of website that allows users to easily add and edit content (Leuf and Cunningham, 2001). It is a simplification of the process of creating HTML web pages combined with a system that records each individual change that occurs over time, so that at any time, a page can be reverted to any of its previous states. A wiki system thus allows anyone with a web browser to easily edit and create webpages.

The GOP uses Mediawiki, the same technology used by Wikipedia. Wikipedia, a popular end-user editable online encyclopedia, has been described as an environment where knowledge building often takes place (Bryant et al., 2005). It is also among the most prolific collaborative authoring projects ever sustained in an online environment (Bryant et al., 2005). Its success as a tool for supporting knowledge building can be partly explained by certain features normally absent in other wiki implementations. Mediawiki allows registered users to maintain "watchlists" of pages they wish to pay attention to. Users are notified whenever a page on their watchlist is edited. This feature allows users to keep track of the changes that a page might go through. Another feature is the "talk page". Talk pages are secondary webpages, one for each primary page, where users can discuss issues surrounding the topics of the primary pages. Should certain content be added, deleted, or moved elsewhere? Talk pages can support the process of knowledge building by providing a space for users to discuss the knowledge they are creating. Also, novice users can use these pages to understand the evolution of a certain page and understand how consensus was achieved regarding the current state of a page.

The medium of knowledge building discussions is important. Features such as talk pages and watchlists help mitigate many of the challenges to knowledge building, such as dealing with conceptual discussions that are "left in the air" (Cummings, 2003). Talk pages are also different from threaded discussions, which can be problematic since they have no systematic way of promoting convergence of ideas (Stahl, 2001). In the case of Wikipedia, some researchers hypothesize its success lies in how it encourages community introspection: it is strongly designed so that members watch each other, talk about each other's contributions, and directly address the fact that they must reach consensus (Viegas et al., 2004). Through participation in a resource like this, even novices to the Game Ontology have direct access to the practices, discussions, and reasoning of the game studies researchers that use it. Having the Game Ontology on a wiki-enabled web site also provides opportunities for people outside of the project to easily participate. There are many legitimate opportunities to help build knowledge in the ontology. Not only are there numerous entries that are lacking in depth and examples, but there are also entire areas that haven't been explored. In summary, the technology platform supporting the GOP affords knowledge building by:

1. Providing separate spaces for content and content discussion
2. Providing visibility of the discussions and process behind the creation of content
3. Helping users keep track of content they are interested or involved in

Study

In early 2007, the Game Ontology was used as part of the regular activities in an introductory game design class. The class was an undergraduate lecture-style class with over 200 students. In the class, students were required to play and design games, read scholarly articles, and turn in written assignments. Participants were recruited at the beginning of the term, and 81 students chose to participate.

Data Collection and Analysis

As part of their regular coursework, students were introduced to some terminology from the GOP. Three weeks later students were asked to complete a game ontology assignment. For the assignment, students had to pick two games they knew well. Then they had to find entries in the ontology and edit them in such a way as to add those games as examples (strong or weak). Students had to edit at least two entries (ex: game A as a strong example of one entry and weak example on another, and vice versa for game B), but they could edit up to four different entries. The only additional restriction was that at least two of the examples should be added to entries under the "Rules" sub-hierarchy.

Students were graded only on the completion of the assignment. Because it is often the case that disagreements about examples has led to the refinement of the ontology, grading did not focus on the correctness of the examples. Additionally, students were offered the possibility of extra credit for participation that went above and beyond the assignment requirements, such as meaningful contributions to existing entries, proposing new entries, and participating in discussions on the talk page. The researchers were not involved in the assessment, though they did participate in the discussions that took place on the ontology wiki pages. The duration of the assignment was officially one week, though students could begin their participation sooner.

Only 49 of the 81 students that signed up to participate in the study contributed to the game ontology, one of the final assignments in the class. The instructor noted the drop-off in participation, "I did notice that a fair number of students didn't actually do the Game Ontology Project assignment. It seemed like many students missed that last one and many students seemed to miss the other final assignments. Due to the duration of class and due to the other assignments that we had, I got the sense that students tended to fall behind." For many students, like Violet, the amount of class work near the end of the term forced them to focus on assignments they felt were more important, "I think I didn't do it actually. Yeah, I was swamped by this project from another class, oh, and the project from [this] class as well." I did not find evidence of more substantive reasons to explain the drop-off in student participation.

In terms of the changes made to the ontology, a total of 381 edits were made. Edits varied from very minor (one or two characters, such as when correcting a typo) to one or two paragraphs in length. In total, 65 different ontology entries were edited, and participants contributed a total of 128 different examples. Additionally, I conducted interviews with sixteen students, three of the teaching assistants, and the instructor. As in my other studies, I employed theoretical sampling. This means that cases are chosen based on theoretical (developed *a priori*) categories to provide polar types, rather than for statistical generalizability to a larger population (Eisenhardt, 1989). Interview subjects were selected based on their level of prior experience with games (novice, intermediate, gamer) and participation on the GOP (none, minimum required, active participation). All interviews were audio-recorded and transcribed. In addition to asking students about their experience participating in the ontology, our interview protocol includes questions about potential challenges of learning about games. The student protocol also includes open-ended questions about their expectations regarding the course and changes they would make to the assignments. Interviews were semi-structured to ensure that all participants are asked certain questions yet still allow them to raise other issues they feel are relevant. Data from the interviews was used to contextualize and provide insight to the analysis of student participation. All interviewee names appearing in this chapter have been changed for reasons of privacy.

I also analyzed the quality of contributions made by the students. Three subject matter experts were asked to evaluate a random selection of examples written by the students. The subject matter experts were selected due to their prior experience working as researchers on the Game Ontology Project. The goal of this evaluation was to determine whether or not their contributions were valuable, i.e., should the example remain in the ontology? I also wanted to get a sense of how these contributions could be characterized.

Of the 128 examples written, the experts evaluated a randomly selected sample of 96. Assuming a normal distribution, this sample size is representative of the larger population for a 95% confidence level and 5% margin of error. Each expert independently reviewed 32 different examples. Additionally, for purposes of calculating interrater reliability, a separate random sample of ten examples was independently evaluated by all three experts. As recommended by Lombard et al (2002), two indices were selected to determine interrater reliability. In terms of percent of agreement, two of the three raters agreed 100% of the time and all three agreed 60% of the time. Fleiss' kappa (1971) was calculated as 0.87. According to Neuendorf, from a review of "rules of thumb" set out by several methodologists, "coefficients of 0.90 or greater would be acceptable to all, 0.80 or greater would be acceptable in most situations, and the criterion of 0.70 is often used for exploratory research. (Neuendorf, 2002)" More liberal criteria are usually used for the indices known to be more conservative, such as Fleiss' kappa (Lombard et al., 2002). Thus, in the case of this research, a value of 0.87 is considered acceptable.

In the following sections, where appropriate, I will describe how my observations and findings illustrate students' understanding of videogames according to the four contexts for understanding games I defined in Chapter 3.

Samples of Student Participation

I will now present and briefly discuss two contributions made by different students for the same Ontology entry. One of the examples was evaluated positively by the experts and the other was not. My goal isn't to comment on the insight, quality, or general correctness of the contributions. Those issues will be discussed later in the context of the experts' analysis.

<u>Checkpoint</u>

Checkpoints, as defined in the ontology, "are specific (non random and predetermined) places or moments in a game wherein a player is not forced to start completely over if he or she were to lose a chance. This, of course, only applies to those games where the loss of a chance implies having to begin anew (instead of continuing at the place and moment in which the chance was lost). The use of a checkpoint enables the player to start automatically at the checkpoint that is closest to the ending and has been activated or visited.

Different games have different mechanisms for the "activation" of checkpoints. Checkpoints are usually activated simply by reaching them or by explicitly interacting with an object that represents the checkpoint within the level. Each level can have multiple checkpoints." The Checkpoint entry is a low-level entry (i.e., it has no children) and its parent entry is Gameworld Rules.

In the following example, the student describes how checkpoints have been implemented in *Super Mario World 2: Yoshi's Island*. The example also notes how this implementation has additional effects on gameplay (e.g.,. "give 5 extra seconds") that are not considered in the original Ontology definition.

This entry was evaluated positively by the expert reviewers, though they said parts of it should be rewritten for clarity and brevity.

> "*Super Mario World 2: Yoshi's Island is a strong example of the checkpoint system. During the levels players encounter 'star hoops', which once jumped through, save the players position in the level at that point. If you die, you are brought back to this point, and there are mutiple star hoops throughout each level which save you place as long as you jump through them. These hoops also increase you star number, or the amount of time you have to retrive the crying baby mario (a clock counts down when you are injured and mario has been displaced, indicacting how many seconds you have to retrive him or essentialy lose a life and start over) - Once you jump through the hoop you are give 5 extra seconds to this time, but only once. So if you die, or lose baby Mario, you are still brought back this spot in the level. It is possible to play past levels, but previous completions of a level do not affect where you star out in the level.*" – **Super Mario World 2: Yoshi's Island (strong example)**

In the following example, presented as a weak example, the author argues that *Tekken 5* does not really have checkpoints. The author explains what happens when the player-controlled character dies in the game, and notes how this is different from the definition of checkpoint. This example was not evaluated positively by the expert evaluators, though it was noted that this example drew the expert to think about improvements that could be made to the Ontology entry.

> "There are no real checkpoints in the main game because when a character dies during the arcade mode, they are just prompted to press start before the timer runs out and that person has another go at the stage where they died on. These "Continue?" screens are not a checkpoint because they can appear anywhere along the way in arcade mode and not in specific locations as there are no real locations in the game." – **Tekken 5 (weak example)**

Results

Overall effects and Student Perception

In general, the students were positive about the role they felt the GOP played in the context of the class. Anne felt that "it was a good assignment because it really made you think and try and really think about the aspects of the games you had played."

For the majority of the students, the ontology was a source of definitions. Bert describes that "there were a lot of times where [the instructor] would just be rattling away all these terms, and I would be a little bit scared in my seat, and I would write down what I didn't understand, and I would go home and check it out." Many of these students didn't perceive the GOP as a "living" source with definitions that could be debated, edited and improved.

On the other hand, some students found that using the GOP broadened their understanding of games. Frank noted that "I didn't really think about games along those terms before, and it was nice to have a new perspective on games." Understanding games as the combinations of structural elements of gameplay was novel to them. Anne comments that she "thought the categories were really interesting. I hadn't thought about the breakdown of games before, so I really liked that." Finally, some students felt it was helpful to them in the context of their game design projects. Joe felt that "when you're making a game, there a lot of choices you have to make, and knowing your options made your choices clearer."

Other studies have shown that even though online resources may be public, they will not necessarily be perceived as public by those that are using them (Hudson and Bruckman, 2005; Forte and Bruckman, 2006). This was not the case in my research. Students realized that their participation on the ontology would be visible to people outside of the class as well as the games researchers that regularly worked on the ontology. They realized they were making changes and adding content to a public resource, and that their work had consequences beyond the assignment. In this sense, the assignment was an authentic and legitimate activity.

Mary noted that "I was sort of worried about putting something in that wouldn't fit because it is an editable site, and so I would put something in, and it would be like...oh that's really wrong, I'm going to mess things up for the game researchers." Mike, on the other hand, described how he was concerned with the correctness of his examples because "if somebody were to have put things in categories that they didn't belong, and they weren't corrected, then they might have learned to opposite of what's true."

Navigation and Participation

I hypothesized that the hierarchical structure would prove beneficial to students participation and understanding of the ontology. For many students, this was in fact their primary way of browsing the ontology, and they often started with the entries suggested by the instructor.

However, I found evidence of other popular ways of navigating. Dave describes how "there's a list sorted by alphabetical order, and I just looked through which ones looked more interesting to me" while Chris opted to "just randomly bring a page, just any random page. And this is how I navigated through that because I wasn't really sure what I wanted to add." In addition to a hierarchical style of navigation, students made use of random and indexed navigation.

The choice of navigation is tied to the way that students approached the task of adding strong and weak examples. Some students approached the game ontology with a specific game in mind and then tried to identify entries for which they could use that game as an example (strong or weak).

The other approach was to start from an entry they found particularly interesting or compelling and then try to come up with examples (weak and strong) for it. Students with a game in mind favored indexed and random navigation, while those focused on the entries found the hierarchical scheme more useful.

Supporting Deeper Understanding

Student participation in the GOP also seemed to afford a deeper understanding of videogames according to the contexts outlined in Chapter 3: games in culture (1st context), games and other games (2nd context), games and technology (3rd context), and deconstruction and components (4th context).

Since the purpose of the GOP is to define and organize important structural elements of games, it is perhaps ideally suited for the 4th context of understanding games. Unsurprisingly, I found evidence to support the idea that students are beginning to understand games in this context. As I will explain later, the use of strong and weak examples was especially productive.

Although I didn't find significant evidence of supporting understanding games in the context of culture (first context), there is evidence for the two remaining: games and other games (second context) and games and technology (third context).

In the following example, the contributor argues that *Randomness*[16] is present in *Baldur's Gate* in the way that attacks are resolved. The example notes that *Baldur's Gate's* rules system is based on another game whose attacks are resolved by rolling dice. The author of this example is demonstrating an understanding of aspects of *Baldur's Gate* in context with other games (2nd context).

> *"In the computer role-playing game Baldur's Gate, the success of a player character's attack is determined probabilistically by rolling a 20-sided dice. Since the rules-system is based on a well-known paper and pencil role-playing game (Dungeons and Dragons), it can be assumed that the players are aware of the probabilities involved."* **– Baldur's Gate (strong example)**

I also hypothesized that the use of strong and weak examples would prompt students to reflect on games at a deeper level. Tom discusses that the game *The Elder Scrolls IV: Oblivion* forced him to explore some issues more deeply.

> *"It was really challenging to come up with specifically strong and weak examples of things because there were some of them that you could come up with gray areas for. In Oblivion, depending on which version of the game you have, you may get a strong ending or a world exhaustion [referring to the entry Game Ends and its child entry Gameworld Exhaustion], because if you have the PC version you could download more pieces or more modules to increase your game time, and those are all part of the world. So in a sense, the world never really ends."* **- Tom**

---

[16] Randomness is described in the Game Ontology Project as: "the results or resolution of certain events or actions are determined in a probabilistic manner. The probability may or may not be known to the player. Randomness is also known as chance." This entry is a low-level entry (i.e., it has no children entries) whose parent entry is Gameplay Rules.

The use of strong and weak examples in the Ontology helped some students think more deeply about the entries and how they relate to what they see in certain games. In general, they achieved a more nuanced understanding. While coming up with strong examples was generally considered easy by most students, having to identify weak examples and justify their reasoning elicited greater reflection and discussion. Tom's example is also illustrative of how he begins to understand games more deeply. Tom began to consider *Oblivion* in the 3rd context (games and technology). Here he comments on how the platform on which the game is executed changes the game. Additionally, he is considering two versions of the game, thus also foregrounding issues of the 2nd context (games with respect to other games). Orville also commented how participating in the Ontology made him consider issues of the 3rd context, "I found it interesting that it wasn't just about the software. It was also about the interface and the hardware which I found is an integral part of the game experience. I hadn't thought about that."

In the following weak example for the entry *Lives*,[17] the contributor explains how in *Legend of Zelda: A Link to the Past* there is a health system that isn't represented like other games that have strong examples of *Lives*. However, there is a non-central game mechanic, capturing a healing fairy in a bottle, which is functionally similar to how Lives work. This example highlights how achieving a deeper understanding of games in the 4th context (deconstruction and components) entails more than just identifying components, but actually understanding how they work and what role they play. In the example below, there is a functional, rather than representational, similarity, thus making for a valuable and insightful example in the Ontology.

> "In Legend of Zelda: A Link to the Past, fairies have healing powers. 'Touching' a fairy will restore some of Link's hearts [the player controlled character], but the fairies can also be captured by use of the bee net. If Link possesses an empty bottle, the fairy can be stored in the bottle for later release/use as normal. Additionally, if a bottled fairy exists in Link's inventory upon depletion of hearts, Link will die, but be immediately resurrected with half of his maximum hearts filled, and gameplay continues. If no fairy is present, the player must reload from a save point. This is a weak example of Lives because Zelda does not have an explicit

---

[17] (abbreviated) Lives represent a measure of opportunities that a player has to succeed in the game. Expenditure (or loss) of a life implies a break in gameplay as opposed to a continuous gameplay experience in which certain attributes may decrease over time. For example, if the character the player controls a shield which is able to take damage (and disappear), it should not be considered a life, since the players' gameplay experience is not interrupted when, say, a missile hits the shield and disappears. The break in gameplay is usually accompanied by a representation of the loss incurred. For example, an animation of the player-controlled avatar falling to the ground in a faint.

representation of this concept, the hearts representing Link's health in a similar fashion to Half-Life's health bar. However, when the player has captured a fairy and dies, the resurrection is functionally very similar to what happens in regular games with lives. In this sense, the fairy in the bottle is equivalent to Link having an extra "life" stored away." **(weak example)**

Challenges

There are many barriers to eliciting participation and collaboration on wiki environments (Guzdial et al., 2002), and our study was not an exception. Many students were not familiar with wikis and the features offered by Mediawiki. This confusion led students to possibly fail to understand that regardless of their activity, the wiki site still contains all the information necessary for grading the assignment. When asked why he didn't edit other people's contributions, Chris comments that "if somebody had put that there, and that was their contribution, then it might not be a good idea to move it for the sake of their grade. If I moved it, it would look like they didn't put something."

Forte and Bruckman (2007) have noted that instructors can find it challenging to assessing collaborative wiki work. So, an alternate hypothesis for understanding students' reticence to collaborate on the wiki is that students believed that removing content from a page would affect the teaching assistants' ability to grade the assignments. Also, having one assignment may have limited the possibilities of students engaging more with the discussions surrounding the entry definitions and value of certain examples. For many students, completing the assignment was an issue of "fire and forget", as there was little incentive to return to the ontology, read what their classmates may have added and possibly refine knowledge created on the site.

Improving the assignment can help with some of this. For example, the assignment could be changed to encourage continued participation. Another approach could be to try similar, but shorter, assignments and have students engage with the GOP more fully over the whole of the course.

A broader issue is how to help students move from viewing knowledge as static and "given" to something that they can help create and define. Essentially, there is a tension between becoming familiarized with the vocabulary, ideas, and concepts in the ontology and realizing that you are participating in refinining, defining those same concepts. For many students, this wasn't a distinction they could articulate. When asked about whether he considered making changes or edits to an entry, and not just adding examples, Joshua recalls "I hadn't thought of that. I guess people could, but then you wouldn't have these standard terms, right?" Kyle also brought up the issue of standardization and positioned his participation in the ontology as one that should reinforce, rather than challenge the status quo of existing definitions, "it's interesting that you standardize terms and that you have specific examples for each term and I guess that we [the students] come in to help shore up the walls or fill in the blanks."

There are alternate hypotheses that might explain students' view of the ontology as static. One is that the way in which the ontology was presented to students may have misled students into assuming a static view of knowledge. Also, students might have viewed their participation in the GOP as peripheral and that, since they were not central members of the project, they were not qualified, or ready, to participate more centrally. However, further evidence is necessary to support these hypotheses.

Contributions to Game Studies

The expert evaluation of the examples written by the students was quite positive. The experts determined that 60% of the examples should remain in the ontology while only 14.5% should be removed (see Table 11). For the remaining examples (25.5%), the experts were ambivalent. Most of the examples, including those the experts thought should remain in the ontology, were judged to need further proofreading and editing. Others could be improved by providing further information that better contextualizes the example with respect to the entry where it appears. For instance, one expert notes, for an example added to the "Boss Challenge" entry (see Table 9), "[I] would like a little more detail on the structure of the 'town' and 'gym leader' situation for those of us who are Pokémon-challenged. I'm guessing you fight people in the town and work your way up to the 'gym leader' boss." Other examples could benefit from the removal of unnecessary commentary or editorial such as the opinion of the relative merits of a game over its sequel. "There's valuable info here, just a little noise around the signal", notes one of the experts (see Table 10). The expert reviewers also found some examples (10% of all examples) that should be changed from strong examples to weak examples or vice versa.

Table 9: User submitted example lacking enough detail

Boss Challenge (Pokémon)
Pokémon is a strong example of a game with Boss Challenges. Usually in every town, the player must defeat the gym leader. Each gym leader has different types of Pokémon such as Water or Fire and different strategies are necessary for defeating each one.

The results of the evaluation were also positive, even when considering only those examples that should be removed. Few examples were considered "non-salvageable" (only 6% of all examples) because they were incorrect or did not apply to the particular ontology entry where they were included. More than half (56%) of those examples evaluated as "should be removed" were considered relevant, but not worth the effort to correct. One of the experts noted, "Sometimes the students didn't seem to find the right words and simply explained the examples very poorly. I found 2 types of 'bad' examples, the least of these were those that were not relevant. Most were relevant but poorly explained."

Table 10: User submitted example with extraneous information

Character Customization (NBA Shootout 2005)
NBA Shootout 2005 provides the player with a flood of features of customization for his or her character. When you start customizing you can first choose the height of your player which also correlates to which position that you would choose. You wouldn't like to put a 5' 4" player in a post position. After you are allowed to choose what skin color you want, color of your eyes, and all the aspects to your uniform that you want. The feature that allows you the most fun though is the feature that allows you to control the body parts of the player. If you want the player to have huge hands, go on ahead. The game allows you to control every aspect of customization which makes this game a strong example of character customization.

When characterizing the contribution made by the examples added by the students, perhaps the single most common feature was that the examples helped add variety to the ontology (58% of all examples). In this case, the criterion for variety was determined at the level of each individual entry. In other words, does the example add variety to the entry in which it appears? Of the examples that added variety, 79% refer to a game that many people have played or know about (46% of all examples), thus making the entry more accessible. When trying to understand a particular entry, it is helpful to have a variety of examples that refer to well-known or popular games so that people are likely to find a game they can relate to their personal experiences.

Variety was also increased through the addition of examples that refer to games that are unusual or rare, yet still important for people to know about. This was the case of 21% of the examples that added variety, in other words, 12% of all examples. Examples that refer to games that are unusual or rare can help broaden students' understanding by drawing attention to games they might not have heard about or considered playing otherwise. Many of these "rare" games are interesting, from a game studies perspective, because they can help illustrate the nuances and varying interpretations that an ontological entry can have (Zagal et al., 2007).

Table 11: Expert evaluation of student contributions

Expert Evaluation	Percentage
Example should remain in the ontology	60%
Ambivalent about permanence or removal of example	25.5%
Example should be removed from the ontology	14.5%

As described previously, the majority of the examples provided by the students served simply as contributions to the body of knowledge that is the game ontology (see Table 11). But some students' examples also contributed to the field. The expert evaluators noted that some examples (5%) helped them realize something they hadn't noticed or thought about previously. One expert commented "I wasn't expecting to find examples of that entry from that particular genre of games. I wasn't really aware of how that genre had evolved and I guess I should play some more!"

Also, 9.1% of the examples helped the experts notice something about the ontology entry that needed to be improved or expanded upon. For example, in the entry "Games Ends", one of the students added a weak example referring to the game Pac-Man. Pac-Man, in theory, does not have a formal ending (you can't win, it just gets harder and harder until you lose). However, there is a notorious technical issue that causes the game to crash when the player reaches the 256th screen (Sellers, 2001).

The student-provided example draws attention to an issue that was not considered in the original entry (game ends due to technical issue) and made the expert wonder if the entry should be modified to account for this.

Another example, this time for the ontology entry "Agent Goals", made an expert realize an implicit bias in the entry. "The way the entry is written, it sounds like we're talking about states in state machine AI. What we're getting at in the end here is that AI-controlled agents have a prioritized set of goals that they seek to fulfill (like a hierarchical goal tree and the agents can switch modes between those goals according to the hierarchy of the goal tree)?" The entry, as written, implicitly assumes certain details about how agent goals are implemented in videogames, and the expert wonders whether or not we want to leave the entry with that bias.

Student examples also served as a catalyst for reflection on broader issues of the game ontology. Experts indicated that 2.7% of the examples helped them think about something that should be added to another part of the ontology. For instance, an example referring to the game *Katamari Damacy* was added to the entry *To Remove*.[18] In this game, the player controls a large sticky ball that is rolled around. As the ball rolls over items these become stuck to the ball, causing the ball to grow, thus being able to roll over larger items, and so on. The game also maintains a record of all of the items a player has ever rolled over that spans all of the times a player has ever played the game. The expert noted that this was an interesting case of in-game/out-of-game interactions. This is something the expert felt hasn't really been addressed directly in the Ontology.

These examples drew attention to future areas of growth for the ontology, including new directions to pursue or new entries that should be added. In other words, student participation was more than just an "efficient" way of generating new examples, it also helped propel experts' thinking in new directions.

In summary, I am confident in stating that the students' contributions to the ontology were not only useful to them, pedagogically speaking, but can also be fairly characterized as legitimate contributions to a body of knowledge that is part of the academic field of game studies.

Discussion

One of the challenges for this study was answering how to make the GOP, and the terms and concepts it describes, approachable and useful to students. I also wanted to help students leverage knowledge they have about videogames. From that perspective, I believe this experience was a success. Many students chose to participate beyond the minimum requirement. For instance, 28% of the students used more than two games and 34% edited more than four ontology entries.

The GOP was approachable by the students, and they also felt it played an important role in the context of their games education. Fran describes, "If you're going to study game design, it's important to have standardized terminology. I think that with the game ontology wiki it's interesting that you standardize terms and that you have many specific examples for each term, and that's very important in terms of understanding the different parts that make a game or different aspects from different games." I also wondered if the student contributions would be meaningful, or useful, to the game ontology project itself. On this point, I feel that I have succeeded in providing a learning environment where students were able to legitimately contribute to an emergent field of study.

---

[18] (abbreviated) Entities have the ability to destroy other entities in the game world. When an entity is removed, it ceases to exist in the game world, but the removal or absence of the entity may affect the game world. Removal is the opposite of creation.

However, some students' misperception of the game ontology as a static and monolithic source is an issue that needs further exploration. In particular, I wonder if having students provide examples only reinforced the definitions provided in the ontology rather than encouraging them to challenge those definitions. Student-provided examples helped the subject matter experts reflect and think in new directions; this is something that ideally the students should also engage in. Further work is required to look at how to achieve the delicate balance between reinforcing and building upon existing ideas and challenging the status quo in such a way as to promote new ideas. Also, it is not clear to us how many students participated less due to concerns of "messing things up." In this sense, the legitimacy and authenticity of the assignment may have also acted as a barrier to participation.

Finally, there is an issue regarding sustainability and scalability of this approach. Are the positive results of this experience the result of students being able to take advantage of the "low-hanging fruit"? If I were to repeat this experience, how many entries would become saturated with a too many similar examples that only marginally help illustrate an entry? This concern can be addressed by making changes to the structure of the game ontology to support larger numbers of examples or provide users with tools to filter the information provided. Users could filter the examples for an entry so as to only display examples that refer to games for a certain hardware platform or display examples of games released after a certain year. However, the nature of the medium also helps mitigate the "too many examples" problem. Older games are frequently unknown to younger students and are also often inaccessible due to technical reasons such as hardware obsolescence. The Game Ontology Project will always need to update the examples to remain accessible and understandable to its users and to allow new games to force the re-evaluation of existing entries.

An additional way of introducing the Game Ontology Project would be to encourage students to create and define ontology entries before being formally introduced to the project. Students could then, given the entries they have written, see whether there are already similar entries in the ontology and discuss the differences. If there are no similar entries, students could add their new entries as proposed ones. This exercise would be similar to one used by Holopainen and colleagues when they teach game design using design patterns (Holopainen et al., 2007).

In summary, I feel that this experience shows that it is possible to design learning environments that are approachable by learners, allow them to contribute legitimately to external communities of practice, and support visibility and access to the practices of a broader community. However, it is important to carefully consider not only the affordances of the technology but also the practices of the broader community in which students will participate. Navigating these issues is crucial so that students may effectively engage in practices meaningful to them as well as the broader community.

In this chapter, I explored two questions: (Q3) How can we help students leverage knowledge from personal experiences with games to create abstract and deeper knowledge?, and (Q4) What role can novices play in a professional knowledge-building community of practice? In answer to these questions, I have demonstrated the use of wikis for facilitating legitimate novice participation in a knowledge-building community of practice (Q3). I have shown how the Game Ontology Wiki can provide a space for the meaningful and legitimate use of experiential knowledge while affording making connections between abstract concepts and ideas and gameplay experiences. I have also demonstrated the benefits (and challenges) of novice participation in knowledge-building communities of practice (Q4). In particular, I have shown how novices can provide a variety of ideas, both broad as well as specific, that can help push expert thinking in new directions. In the next, and final chapter, I will discuss some of the broader implications of my work as well as outline some future research directions that may be productive to pursue.

CHAPTER 7: DISCUSSION AND CONCLUSIONS

When I began working on this research, I was interested in understanding not only the learning issues involved in learning about games but also in somehow validating and arguing for the importance that games have in today's world. Games have recently been the center of a lot of media attention as a causal factor of a lot of society's ills, including youth violence, child obesity, and social alienation (for an overview of recent media coverage refer to ESA, 2008). Having been interested and engaged with games of multiple shapes and sizes for most of my life, I felt compelled to somehow engage with games on their own terms, support their study, and better understand the role they have played, and may continue to play, in society at large. While many are worried about the "effects" of this new medium, for good or for bad, I have wondered what it means to understand them, and through this, begin to explore the relationships between games, the activity of playing games, and the affordances of this medium for expressing and communicating. My big question has therefore been this: *What does it mean to understand games, and how can we support learners in developing that understanding?*

Table 12 shows the questions I explored to address this question. I began by discussing the importance of achieving a better understanding of the challenges of learning about games (Q1). We know that games aren't necessarily easy to play or easy to learn to play (Gee, 2003; Squire, 2005). We also know that, in general, achieving deep understanding of a domain or subject matter is hard (Bransford et al., 2000). So, what are the particular problems that learners face when learning about games as an expressive medium? What types of challenges will they encounter and how can we address them?

Table 12: Motivating Questions

Q1	What are the challenges of learning about games?
Q2	How can we characterize a naïve understanding of games?
Q3	How can novices leverage knowledge from their personal experiences with videogames to create abstract and deeper knowledge about the medium of videogames, and what may we generalize from this?
Q4	What role can novices play in a professional knowledge-building community of practice?

My initial question (Q1) motivated the importance of understanding the initial understandings and misconceptions that learners may have about games (Q2) and also suggested ideas and possible avenues for addressing the challenges identified. In particular, given the fact that most students have extensive prior experience playing videogames, I chose to explore how we can help learners leverage that knowledge and experience to help them achieve a deeper understanding of videogames (Q3). I chose to explore my third question through the design and use of two online learning environments: GameLog and the Game Ontology Wiki. The idea behind GameLog is to explore how we can support students in getting more out of their experiences with games. In other words, given that students learning about games usually play games, how can we help them improve the potential for learning and deeper understanding of games as an expressive medium that those experiences may have? The idea behind the Game Ontology Project is to explore how we can support students in getting more out of their game experiences. In other words, can their knowledge of games be turned into a resource that may benefit others, as well as themselves? In this last case, I also wanted to explore some of the implications and challenges of providing learners with the opportunity to contribute legitimately contribute to an ongoing game studies research project. In particular, I was interested in exploring the role that novices might play in a professional knowledge-building community of practice (Q4).

In the following sections I will revisit each of the questions I posed and discuss my findings and contributions for each.

Answers to Questions

Q1: What are the challenges of learning about games?

To explore this question, I conducted a qualitative research study in which I performed in-depth interviews with twelve professors and instructors of game studies courses. My results indicate that learning about games can be challenging for multiple reasons. I also found that, in some cases, these challenges also provide opportunities for learning. The general themes I found can be summarized as issues pertaining to the:

1. background of the students,
2. prior experience with videogames,
3. practices and discourse of play,

4. medium of videogames, and the

5. field of game studies.

Issues related to the background of the students

Most students who are taking game classes are drawn to these classes due to their prior and current life experiences with videogames. This means that many game classes attract students from a wide variety of backgrounds. Game classes also attract students who have prior game industry and professional experience, but are looking to complement their years of practical experience with an academic understanding of games. This situation provides the following:

- Challenges for Learning
  - Instructors have a hard time establishing a common level of discourse in class.
  - Students don't necessarily share the same goals.
- Opportunities for Learning
  - Heterogeneity of student backgrounds provides for opportunities to experience different perspectives.
  - In design-based classes, students can bring multiple skills to bear and practice communicational and management skills that will be useful in the workplace.

Issues related to the students' prior experience with videogames

Most students who are taking game classes have extensive prior experience with videogames. Many consider themselves "gamers" or "fans". However, many students' prior experience with videogames, while extensive, are often limited. Students' prior experience with videogames provides the following:

- Challenges for Learning
  - Students have difficulties stepping back from their role as "gamers" or "fans" and reasoning critically, analytically, and taking alternate viewpoints about games.
  - Students find it hard to accept new ideas about games when their judgments are clouded by false assumptions about particular games, game genres, and so on.
  - Students often consider themselves experts in videogames and don't feel they can learn anything new about games, or a game they might have played.

- Students often view game classes as a means for learning how to use the tools for making games, instead of as a means for learning more about games.
- Opportunities for Learning
  - Students' prior experience can have positive effects on motivation, commitment and dedication to the courses.
  - Students' prior knowledge of videogames can provide them with a rich source of knowledge that can add variety and depth to the game class experience.

Issues related to the students' practices and discourse of play

Most students who are taking game classes, due to their extensive prior experience, can rapidly and easily learn to play new games. They have a good feel for gameplay aspects and are also often quite successful at playing games. With regards to their experience surrounding the practice of play, students often encounter the following:

- Challenges
  - Students often confuse being successful at the play of a game with having insight or deep understanding of a game.
  - Students often confuse analyzing a game with listing the features a game may have with their opinion of each.
  - Despite the ease with which students can play games, they often have difficulties expressing ideas about gameplay and articulating their experience with games.
  - Students are generally lacking in models of what appropriate academic or critical discourse surrounding games looks like. Additionally, they lack the vocabulary for describing what they observe and understand.
  - Students find it difficult to learn new modes of play such as playing for analysis or for design.

Issues related to the characteristics and particularities of the medium of the videogame

Videogames have been described as a medium with particular qualities. For example, much has been made of the participatory nature of the medium of videogames (see for example Murray, 1997). This quality, interactivity, could have profound implications. Videogames have also, arguably, played an important role in the development and adoption of computing technology (Burnham, 2001). The technological platforms on which videogames are executed have also rapidly evolved and improved in terms of processing capabilities, storage capacity, graphics, and so on. The characteristics of the medium, together with the technological platform on which they are executed influence learning about videogames in the following ways:

- Challenges
    - "Accessing the content" of a game (i.e. fully experiencing it) requires knowing how to play a game. Students unfamiliar with a game thus need to first learn how to play it before they can begin to deal with other issues.
    - Playing videogames is time-consuming. This makes playing games assigned for classes challenging, especially if there is no prior experience with the game in question.
    - It is often assumed that students have prior experience with the games that will be studied and analyzed in class and it isn't always the case that students will have that experience.
    - Rapidly evolving technological platforms make it challenging to provide access to older games, especially in their original (often obsolete) hardware incarnations.
    - Students' judgment is often clouded by false assumptions and nostalgia related to older games.

Issues related to role and influence of the field of game studies

Game studies is a nascent discipline dedicated to studying digital games and associated phenomena. As an emergent field, it is still in the process of establishing its identity (Mäyrä, 2005), and is wrestling with what its fundamental concepts, ideas, and theoretical models should be. The existence of a formal field of study, together with its newness, plays the following role in learning about games:

- Challenges
    - Professors and instructors are often figuring out what the "fundamentals" are (or should be) and there is a perceived lack of established canon to refer to.
- Opportunities
    - Students feel a great liberty to question and criticize what they read and learn and thus engage in the dialectic and fluid nature of the field.
    - The field of game studies is accessible for participation and also publication.

Q2: How can we characterize a naïve understanding of games?

By synthesizing many of the findings related to the challenges of learning about games, I can provide a characterization of a naïve understanding of games (Q2). Understanding the common misconceptions and initial understandings faced by learners is important if we expect students to learn (Donovan et al., 1999). Furthermore, we can use this knowledge to guide the design of learning environments that leverage and engage learners' misconceptions. For example, cognitive tutors for supporting algebra learning take advantage of the typical problems learners face and use this knowledge to support learners when they make mistakes (Anderson et al., 1995). Linn and colleagues' work on the Knowledge Integration Environment explicitly addressed students' naïve understanding of light in the design of the models they chose to design (Linn et al., 1998). My research contributes to our understanding of how we can support learning about games by providing a characterization of a naïve understanding of games. Summarizing, someone with a naïve understanding of games will often:

1. Confuse being insightful about a game with being successful at playing a game.
2. Describe a game superficially.
   - Focus on the features of a game over describing the rhetoric of a game or the experience of playing it (e.g. "this game has hi-res graphics", "the game has a ton of maps to play").
   - Describe a game judgmentally rather than analytically (e.g., "this game sucks", "this game is cool").
3. Assume that people experience a game the same way they do.
4. Be familiar with specific genres or types of games, but have a narrow view of the medium.
5. Think they can't learn anything new from games they've already played.

This characterization can be used for the design of learning environments for supporting learning about games as well as to address issues regarding the design of curricula in games education.

As with my research on the challenges of learning about games, my characterization of a naïve understanding of games is just a beginning. In further research it would be interesting to explore the potential differences between students who are novices to playing games and those who self-identify as "gamers" or "fans". Do novice game players also share many of the misunderstandings about games that are commonly seen in popular press media (i.e. "games are only for kids")? Further research is also necessary begin to identify the reasons behind some of the evidence for naïve understanding in people learning about games. Do some students naively describe games superficially because of what they read about games? What role, if any, do game reviews play?

Q3: How can novices leverage knowledge from their personal experiences with videogames to create abstract and deeper knowledge about the medium of videogames, and what may we generalize from this?

Given the challenges identified (Q1) and a characterization of a naïve understanding of games (Q2), how can we help learners leverage that knowledge and experience to help them achieve a deeper understanding of videogames (Q3)? Prior experience plays an important and valuable role in learning (Lave and Wenger, 1991; Schank et al., 1999; Bransford et al., 2000). This is particularly so when the learner has personally meaningful connections with what is to be learned as the learner will then engage more attentively (Papert, 1980). Thus, students' extensive personal histories with videogames can be an asset in learning about games. The literature suggests strategies for leveraging experiences such as encouraging reflection and providing new contexts where knowledge from experience can be applied (for an overview, see Bransford et al., 2000). I therefore explored this question through the design and use of two online learning environments: GameLog and the Game Ontology Wiki.

GameLog

GameLog is an online environment designed to support blogging of gameplay experiences. It is designed to support reflective game playing and thus, a deeper understanding of videogames. From a study in which GameLog was used as part of the regular curriculum in two university game classes, I found that blogging about gameplay experiences:

- Affords opportunities for students to reflect on their gameplaying activities.
- Affords personal expression, communication, and collaboration with other students as students share opinions and see what others think.
- Allows students to contextualize their understanding of games.
- Can be an enjoyable experience for students as well as foster a deeper appreciation for games.

I also found that blogging about gameplay affords a deeper understanding of games with respect to the four contexts for understanding games I outlined in Chapter 3: in the context of human culture, other games, the technological platform, and by deconstructing them and understanding their components. Additionally, blogging about gameplay:

- Affords the exploration of multiple perspectives and viewpoints.
- Affords the development of an inquiry of gameplay where students can begin to formulate questions, plans, hypotheses, and investigations they can pursue during their gameplay sessions.

My findings also suggest that the structure of the GameLog assignment played an important role in affording a deeper understanding of games. Students were asked to play a game on three occasions and then write three entries on that experience. I found that writing on multiple occasions encourages students to write different things each time, helps them focus their attention on specific details, provides the opportunity to plan, investigate, and follow up on ideas, and also affords revisiting a game under different lenses. The iterative design of the assignment was thus important in promoting skills and practices that are important for seriously understanding games. In traditional learning environments, students usually get only one chance to "get it right", before moving on to the next assignment. Writing on multiple occasions about the same game helps incorporate iterative practices that have shown useful positive learning benefits in other contexts, such as science learning (Kolodner et al., 1998).

The use of GameLog also highlighted the importance of providing students with multiple opportunities to practice the skills they need to develop together with providing them with occasions to reflect and articulate their ideas at a level that is closer to their observations and experience. It is too often the case that learning activities privilege the end products, like a mid-term report, over the activities that act in support of that end product. Although the quality of the students writing was "informal" in terms of quality (e.g., poor grammar, very informal, etc.), the experience of blogging undoubtedly helped students create the "raw materials" on which their deeper understanding could build upon. In this sense, blogging, as a reflective activity, can help students bridge the gap between experience and understanding.

Game Ontology Wiki

The GOP, which resides on the Game Ontology Wiki, is developing a game ontology that identifies the important structural elements of games, relationships between them, and organizes them hierarchically (Zagal et al., 2007). I conducted a study in which students were invited to participate and contribute to the GOP as part of their regular curriculum. In particular, students were asked to provide examples to existing ontology entries from games they were familiar with. I found that participating in a knowledge-building environment like the GOP:

- Affords opportunities for students to reflect on specific characteristics or aspects of games they have played.
- Provided students with a source for definitions and concepts about games and gameplay.
- Can be an enjoyable experience for students as well as foster a deeper appreciation for games.

I also found that providing strong and weak examples to existing ontology entries affords a deeper understanding of games. Participating in the GOP affords a deeper understanding of games with respect to the three of the four contexts for understanding games I outlined in Chapter 3: in the context of other games, the technological platform, and by deconstructing them and understanding their components. Participating in the GOP facilitates a deeper understanding of games by helping students:

- Establish connections between experiential knowledge of games and the abstract concepts and ideas in the ontology.
- Think about games from the perspective of structural elements of gameplay.

As in earlier research of participation in wiki environments (Guzdial et al., 2002), I found certain challenges that posed barriers to student participation. Despite student familiarity with features of wiki environments, I found that students may not necessarily understand the implications of certain of these features. For example, students often refrained from editing their peers' contributions in fear of adversely affecting the teaching assistant's ability to grade the assignments. Aditionally, some students viewed the knowledge on the ontology as static and "given". In this sense, students interpreted their participation in the ontology as one that should reinforce, rather than challenge the status quo of existing definitions. Although there is some evidence that computer-supported learning environments may help change students' epistemological beliefs (Chan, 1999; Elen and Clarebout, 2001), it is still important that researchers and instructors be aware of the socio-cognitive and socio-cultural factors, including student beliefs and attitudes, that may influence the success of these kinds of learning experiences (Chan and Van Aalst, 2003).

Another important aspect of the students' participation in the GOP has to do with the fact that it was an authentic game studies research project. I will discuss issues of authenticity, legitimacy, and the role student participation played in the ontology in the context of my fourth question.

Q4: What role can novices play in a professional knowledge-building community of practice?

Authentic participation, in the context of learning, has been described as important for promoting learning and deeper understanding (Shaffer and Resnick, 1999). In the context of a knowledge-building community such as the Game Ontology Wiki, what exactly constitutes authentic participation? From Lave and Wenger's characterization of the role of novices in professional communities of practice, we get the notion that novices engage in menial activities that are important and necessary to the community (Lave and Wenger, 1991).

I conducted a study in which students were invited to participate and contribute to the GOP as part of their regular curriculum. In particular, students were asked to provide examples to existing ontology entries from games they were familiar with. With regard to the role novices played as part of this experience, I found that:

- Students felt they contributed meaningfully to the ontology.
- Students contributed legitimately to the ontology by adding knowledge that enriched the Game Ontology.
- Students contributed legitimately to the ontology by helping push expert thinking in new directions.

Other Issues and Findings

Over the course of this research I have encountered other issues and findings that don't fit as cleanly or neatly under the umbrella of the specific questions I outlined earlier. In the following sections I outline some of these.

Motivation

The attraction kids feel towards playing games is often cited as one of the reasons for studying and understanding them. If we could somehow leverage the motivational power of games for the purposes of improving our schools, learning "wouldn't be a problem". Some of the earliest research on the use of videogames for learning focused on identifying and characterizing the intrinsically motivating qualities of videogames (Malone, 1980; Malone, 1981; Cordova and Lepper, 1996).

Unfortunately, as Joseph and Nacu noted (2003), the medium by itself generally isn't enough. Games aren't necessarily easy to play or easy to learn to play (Gee, 2003; Squire, 2005). Squire, for example, found when introducing the strategy game Civilization III into curricula, that "students were anything but immediately motivated. In part, this lack of motivation resulted from the fact that most students needed six to seven hours of gameplay to understand even the most basic game concepts.

Although after-school students were less resistant and more motivated to learn the game, roughly 25% of students in school situations complained that the game was too hard, complicated, and uninteresting, and they elected to withdraw from the gaming unit and participate in reading groups instead (Squire, 2005)."

So, what role does motivation play in the context of learning about games? In my research, I found that students who choose to learn about games generally are interested in them and also have considerable background experience and personally meaningful connections to games. These characteristics, in principle, are an ideal combination. However, as in Squire's findings (Squire, 2005), I found that motivation cannot, and should not, be considered a "silver bullet" with the power to engage students and help keep them "focused on their learning".

Regardless of the activity or the medium, motivation is something that will wax and wane. In a learning environment there are simply too many issues, all of them interrelated, for it to be possible to isolate one and hope to solve everything. Motivation is one ingredient among many. In many cases, addressing a lack of motivation may be the first thing that needs to be addressed. However, for a learning environment to be successful, a host of other ingredients also need to be in place in the right amounts.

Expertise

When I approached this research, I assumed that students studying and learning about videogames were experts on videogames. Studying expert videogame players as they learned about games seemed an interesting scenario to explore, and I was curious about the possible challenges they might face.

When I conducted the preliminary study on the challenges faced by students learning about videogames, I was surprised by the challenges students faced. Summarizing:

- An expert player isn't necessarily more insightful, and might even be less so than a novice player.
- Expert players are often blind to broader issues of videogames.
- Player's expertise is often very specific, limited to certain types of games, and often full of gaps.
- Expert players aren't often comparable to each other due to the wide variety of games, game types, skills required to play, and technological platforms they are familiar with.

The expertise students had was often counter-productive and hindered their learning more than it helped them. While this raises challenges for the instructors, it also raises the question of what expertise, exactly, these students have. There is a need for a more nuanced perspective of what we mean by "game expert".

Crowley and Jacobs (2002) define an island of expertise as "any topic in which children happen to become interested and in which they develop relatively deep and rich knowledge." Perhaps "expert gamers" could be considered as having some sort of island of expertise surrounding videogames? Crowley and Jacobs suggest that these areas of connected interest and understanding create "abstract and general themes" that become the basis of further learning, both within and around the original topic area, and potentially in domains further afield. However, what would those abstract and general themes be in the case of games?

As I described in Chapter 4, students are often experts at playing games and have considerable knowledge of how to interact with games. However, the islands of expertise built around game playing do not necessarily connect with discourse and deep understanding of game studies.

College-age students learning about videogames are significantly different than the children Crowley and Jacobs describe. Islands of expertise, they argue, develop as the culmination of a long series of collaborative interactions that are opportunistic and relatively unremarkable when viewed individually, but which collectively create a powerful linkage between understanding and interest (Crowley and Jacobs, 2002). These islands of expertise are constructed using explanatoids: short fragments of explanatory talk, typically between parent and child.

In the case of videogame experts, this explanatory talk probably arises from communication with peers as well as from people they interact with while playing games. It would be interesting to track what game players learn in this way. It would also be interesting to explore what kinds of islands of expertise develop when one has a game designer or a games studies scholar as a parent or companion while playing. More research is still necessary to better understand the types of knowledge that videogame experts have and how this knowledge was created.

Conclusions

Having re-visited my findings for each of my questions, I now return to my main motivating question: What does it mean to "understand" games and how can we support learners in developing that understanding?

The medium of games is developing at a rapid pace. Many of the games currently available on the market would have been inconceivable, technically and creatively, ten years ago. Developing a deep understanding of videogames can be likened to chasing a moving target, since ideas and notions of what games are and what meanings they can convey are continually being challenged and negotiated. It only takes one new game to radically change your understanding of the possibility space of the medium as a whole. Games that birth new genres and explore novel gameplay ideas are designed, developed, and released at a rate that many would consider alarming. From this perspective, it is perhaps unsurprising that I found that both novice game players as well as "gamers" experienced challenges to understanding games.

Generally speaking, novices at playing games found the issues related to learning about the medium to be more problematic. On the other hand, "gamers" seem to have more issues from their practices and discourse of play as well as their prior experience with videogames. Arguably, the issues faced by novice game players will "go away" as new generations grow up in environments where videogames are increasingly prevalent. In other words, novices to games will become rarer.

However, videogames are changing too much, and too fast, for us to assume that many of the challenges of learning about games will be solved simply by broader exposure to games as a medium. Essentially, many of today's "gamers" are novices with respect to the games that were current 10 years ago. In this sense, the skills, experience, and knowledge they have are quite limited when considering the broader picture of the medium.

Also, given the rapid pace at which the medium is growing and developing, current "gamers" are rapidly "left behind", becoming novices with respect to the newest and latest games.

These issues highlight the importance of looking for solutions that are, for the most part, independent of focusing on supporting learning about games as they are currently understood. Rather, we should explore ways of helping learners make sense of games as they are currently understood while also preparing them to make sense of the games that are yet to be invented. This requires learning better how to help them use their understanding of what currently is to envision and create what could be.

In GameLog, I showed how blogging can be used to help students reflect on their experiences and thus gain new insights from them as well as help them begin to approach future experiences with new perspectives.

In the Game Ontology Wiki, I showed how participating in an ongoing research project by adding new knowledge can be used as a way to help students establish connections between their knowledge and the concepts and ideas developed as part of the research project. By participating in an ongoing project, students could also gain visibility into knowledge building as a way of understanding, and creating new understanding.

However, the experience of adding new knowledge and participating in a knowledge-building enterprise contrasts with the evidence I found supporting the notion that students perceived the ontology as a static source. In particular, this notion seems to contradict the current rhetoric in which youth are becoming "digital" and increasingly accustomed to create, re-create, and re-interpret their experiences with media by mixing, recombining, editing, and mashing-up new artifacts from previous ones (Jenkins, 2006).

So perhaps we were too quick to propose "re-mixing" as a way of understanding and creating new understanding? I think not. There are other explanations for my observations. One possibility is that students viewed their participation in the GOP as peripheral and that, since they were not central members of the project, they were not qualified or ready to participate more centrally.

Students may have perceived that proposing and editing ontology entries was an activity better left to "the experts" rather than appropriately open to all. It is also possible that the "school" context is what essentially misled the students into assuming a static view of knowledge. As Barab and Duffy (2000) describe, "all too frequently, school culture accords knowledgeable skill a reified existence, commodifying it, and turning knowledge into something to be 'acquired'." Further research is needed to better understand whether or not this experience was isolated and what role the object of study (games) and the structure of the assignment may have played.

My work also shows another perspective on the notion of helping learners make sense of games as they are currently understood while preparing them to make sense of the games yet to be invented: help learners by allowing them to help the experts as well. I have shown how we can support an emergent field in defining the language and vocabulary necessary to developing a common understanding of its objects of study. We can do this by allowing novices in the field to participate in knowledge building with experts and also contribute to the growth of the field.

However, we do not know in what ways this result depends on the fact that the field of game studies is new and rapidly evolving. My research indicates that some of the factors that played an important role in this experience include the degree of established theory of the field, the relative experience of the experts, the knowledge and experience of novices with regard to the subject matter, and the personal relevance of the subject matter to the novices' lives. In the case of game studies, we have a field with little established theory concerning subject matter that is close and personal to novices' lives. In this sense, game studies, as a discipline, is "close" to the average "gamer". This "closeness" makes it easier to create spaces of shared discourse where new understandings can be created.

Designing environments that can bring novices and experts together is not trivial. For example, as I discussed in earlier sections, novices often face significant challenges to participation. Kids as Global Scientists (KGS) is an example of an environment that successfully overcomes many of these challenges.

In KGS, students collect local weather data, collaborate with peers and are also mentored by professional scientists (Songer, 1996). In BioKIDS, kids collect information regarding the distribution and behavior of animals in their neighborhood (Parr et al., 2002). The data collected by students in BioKIDS can potentially be used by biologists. In the case of KGS, it isn't clear in what ways the expert mentors may have benefitted from the experience. In BioKIDS, even if student-collected data was used by experts, it isn't clear if the students are aware of what eventually becomes of their work. In each of these projects, demonstrated positive learning effects notwithstanding, there seems to be an unrealized potential for creating a space for meaningful contributions to a broader community or discipline.

Meaningful contributions can be understood as a particular perspective of the term "authenticity" in learning. Shaffer and Resnick found that, in general, there are four "kinds" of authentic learning (1999): (1) learning that is personally meaningful to the learner, (2) learning that relates to the real-world outside school, (3) learning that provides an opportunity to think in the modes of a particular discipline, and (4) learning where the means of assessment reflect the learning process.

Shaffer and Resnick argue for the importance of achieving all of these to promote engagement, learning, and deep understanding. My work has primarily focused on issues related to the first three kinds of authenticity. In particular, I have been able to combine the 2nd and 3rd kinds of authentic learning described above by providing opportunities for learners to contribute to their discipline. This form of authenticity helps establish a connection between the learner and an existing community of practice. If we understand learning as a process of enculturation and identification with a community of practice (Lave and Wenger, 1991), the legitimacy of the contribution a novice may make could be a critical component of the learning experience. It is educationally valuable when novice scientists engage in scientific thinking as scientists do; it can be even more so when they do science that is useful to science itself.

The particular contribution of allowing for meaningful contributions comes from strengthening the ties between learners and novices and a community of practice. The community of practice benefits in two ways: from the contributions made by the novices and, indirectly, from the greater ties and connections that are established between this community and potential future members. The community of practice also benefits from the greater, and stronger, ties it may create with a broader sociocultural environment.

In the same way that the Samba schools of Brazil are successful learning environments due to the tight dialogue they maintain with Brazilian culture and society (Zagal and Bruckman, 2005), emergent fields can be supported by helping them establish these closer ties, provide broader mechanisms for legitimate participation, and allow for greater diversity of its participants.

I argue that GameLog and the Game Ontology Wiki are an example of this kind of support. I also argue that this is, perhaps where the key to supporting understanding and learning about games lies. We know that learning rarely happens in isolation and in a sense, learning is about removing isolation. Learning is about establishing links and bridges. In the case of games, I have discussed the challenges of making connections between personal experiences with games and abstract concepts and ideas. I have also talked about establishing links between the games that exist now, the ones that existed before, and the ones that are yet to exist. Establishing links between novices and experts has also been a theme of my work. Are there other links left to explore? Of course there are. For example, the game industry isn't particularly fond of research academia. Academic work is usually considered dry, overly general, or incompatible with current market trends. Research either discusses concepts that require technology that aren't available for mass-market adoption, or they obsess over gameplay and ideas that are considered dated and thoroughly explored by the industry. How could we support a greater understanding of games by bridging these two communities?

In this sense, having a deep understanding of games is more than being able to analyze games in a meaningful way, know how, and why, games help create certain experiences and evoke certain emotions and feelings in its players. It is also more than knowing how games are used, and can be used, as an expressive medium, or being able to engage in informed discussions on the merits (or lack thereof) of a particular game. Understanding games is about having the ability to establish connections between games and between games and anything else. Supporting learning about games is thus about facilitating these connections.

Future Work

GameLog

As I write this, GameLog is being used as part of the regular coursework of games classes at three different institutions of higher learning. In addition to the need for maintaining the software and ensuring that the site remains functionally usable, this unsolicited and non-advertised interest in the use of GameLog raises a series of questions. How does the way GameLog is used and adopted in each of these classes affect what students learn? What happens when students from each of these different classes, each with different learning goals and pedagogical objectives, interact with each other? What can they discuss with each other? As I noted in Chapter 5, one of GameLog's contributions is that it provides students with the opportunity to share opinions and collaborate in creating a shared understanding. It is an open question whether or not this will continue to happen felicitously when there are significantly more students using the system, and these students don't all share the same educational context and goals.

Additionally, the instructors of the different courses are adapting the assignments in which students use GameLog for the particular needs of their courses. In Chapter 5 I showed that not all the students who use GameLog adopt the same style of entry. Some students write in various prototype styles while others favor one style over others (see Table 7, in Chapter 5, for a summary). When should students be provided with further guidance on how they should write their GameLog entries? What guidance do they need? Should certain styles be favored over others? Can we assume that students are prepared to write in all the styles I observed? Given that course instructors are making adaptations for their particular needs, they might also want to scaffold students adopting certain styles based on their particular learning goals. Currently, GameLog provides an unstructured environment for blogging, and it is an open question how the site can be tailored to simultaneously scaffold the different learning objectives courses may have. For example, some courses aim to support students learning and analyzing elements of gameplay, while others may be more interested in encouraging students to reflect on the narrative and representational aspects of games. In a broader sense, an upcoming research agenda for GameLog lies in exploring ways of providing support for different educational objectives while maintaining the benefits of a larger community of users.

Another agenda for research is exploring and developing ways to support the instructors of these classes. While I have already created some tools and interfaces to assist instructors in assessing their students' participation on GameLog, it is an open question if I can provide instructors with better information regarding students' entries, their activity on the site, and the ways in which they may be participating and interacting with each other. We know that supportig instructors when introducing novel learning environments can be challenging. A particular issue is how to assess student work (Forte and Bruckman, 2007). From this perspective, it would also be interesting to see what features we could leverage from social software (for example, rating systems, media-sharing, micro-blogging) to further scaffold reflection and other meta-cognitive practices.

Game Ontology Project and Wiki

As described in Chapter 6, students who participated in the Game Ontology Wiki often misperceived the game ontology as a static and monolithic source. This is an issue that needs further exploration. In particular, did having students begin to use the system by providing examples reinforce the definitions provided in the ontology rather than encourage them to challenge those definitions? Further work is required to explore ways to achieve the delicate balance between reinforcing and building upon existing ideas while challenging the status quo in such a way as to promote new ideas.

There are also questions regarding finding ways to foster the sustainability and scalability of experiences like those the students had with the Game Ontology. Are the positive results of these experiences the result of students being able to take advantage of the "low-hanging fruit"? If this experience were to be repeated, would the ontology entries become too saturated? As the ontology grows and matures, will it lose some of the qualities it currently has for encouraging novice participation and contributions? What additional ways can we develop to encourage authentic participation? As a broader question, in what ways can we adapt an experience like participating in the Game Ontology Project to other communities and disciplines?

Broader Goals

What can playing videogames teach us about learning, and what can our knowledge about learning teach us about videogames? As a learning scientist, I have followed the recent surge of interest in the use of videogames for educational purposes. Some researchers have argued that certain qualities present in the medium of videogames provide valuable opportunities for learning (Gee, 2003; Shaffer, 2006). These assertions are only just starting to be explored and there are still many open questions. In what ways can we use games to foster deep learning and understanding? In what ways can skills transfer to other domains? I am also interested in exploring the other side of the picture. For instance, what are the potential constraints videogames, as a medium, may place on learning? In my research on learning about videogames, I have found that some traditional challenges to learning, such as lack of student motivation and personally meaningful connections, are reduced. However, students are still challenged by other issues that are negatively impact learning, such as difficulties in reflecting and articulating ideas. Videogames provide a context in which we can study core problems addressed by the learning sciences, such as promoting reflection and meta-cognitive practices. From this perspective, my work can help guide the future exploration of the kinds of learning that videogames encourage and facilitate as well as the challenges in designing games with educational objectives. Similarly, further research is required to better understand what people learn about games from playing them.

REFERENCES

Aarseth, E. (1997). Cybertext : Perspectives on Ergodic Literature. Baltimore, Johns Hopkins University Press.

Aarseth, E. (2001). "Computer Game Studies, Year One." Game Studies 1(1).

Anderson, J. R., A. T. Corbett, K. R. Koedinger and R. Pelletier (1995). "Cognitive Tutors: Lessons Learned." The Journal of the Learning Sciences 4(2): 167-207.

Atkins, B. (2003). More Than a Game: The Computer Game as Fictional Form. Manchester, Manchester University Press.

Avedon, E. M. and B. Sutton-Smith (1971). The Study of Games. NY, London, Sydney, Toronto, John Wiley & Sons.

Baker, J. H. (2003). "The learning log." Journal of Information Systems Education 14(1): 11-13.

Bandura, A. (1986). Social foundations of thought and action: A social cognitive theory. Englewood Cliffs, NJ, Prentice-Hall.

Barab, S., T. Dodge, T. Tuzun, K. Job-Sluder, K. Jackson, C. Arici, J.-S. L., R. J. Carteaux, J. Gilbertson and C. Heiselt (In press). The Quest Atlantis Project: A Socially-Responsive Play Space for Learning. The Educational Design and Use of Simulation Computer Games. B. E. Shelton and D. WIley. Rotterdam, The Netherlands, Sense Publishers.

Barab, S. and T. Duffy (2000). From Practice Fields to Communities of Practice. Theoretical Foundations of Learning Environments. D. Jonassen and S. Land. London, Lawrence Erlbaum Associates.

Barron, B., D. Schwartz, N. Vye, L. Zech, J. D. Bransford and T. C. a. T. G. a. Vanderbilt (1998). "Doing With Understanding: Lessons from Research on Problem- and Project-Based Learning." Journal of the Learning Sciences 7(3&4): 271-310.

Bateman, C. and R. Boon (2006). 21st Century Game Design. Hingham, Mass, Charles River Media.

Bereiter, C. (2002). Education and mind in the knowledge age. Mahwah, NJ, Erlbaum Associates.

Bereiter, C. and M. Scardamalia (1987). The Psychology of Written Composition. Hillsdale, NJ, Lawrence Erlbaum Associates.

Björk, S. and J. Holopainen (2005). Patterns in Game Design. Hingham, Massachusetts, Charles River Media Inc.

Blumenfeld, P. C., E. Soloway, R. W. Marx, J. C. Krajcik, M. Guzdial and A. Palincsar (1991). "Motivating Project-Based Learning: Sustaining the Doing, Supporting the Learning." Educational Psychologist 26(3&4): 369-398.

Bogost, I. (2006). Unit Operations: An Approach to Videogame Criticism. Cambridge, MIT Press.

Bogost, I. (2007). Persuasive Games. Cambridge, Massachusetts, The MIT Press.

Bogost, I. and N. Montfort (2007). New Media as Material Constraint: An Introduction to Platform Studies. 1st International HASTAC Conference, Duke University, Durham NC, April 19-21, 2007.

Bolter, J. D. and R. Grusin (1999). Remediation: Understanding New Media. Cambridge, Massachusetts, The MIT Press.

Bransford, J. D., A. L. Brown and R. R. Cocking (2000). How People Learn: Brain, Mind, Experience, and School (Expanded Edition). Washington, National Academy Press.

Brickhouse, N. W. (1994). "Children's observations, ideas, and the development of classroom theories about light." Journal of Research in Science Teaching 31: 639-656.

Britton, J., N. Burgess, A. MacLeod and H. Rosen (1975). The Development of Writing Abilities. London, Macmillan.

Bruce, C. (1997). The seven faces of information literacy. Adelaide, Auslib Press.

Bruckman, A. (2000). "Situated Support for Learning: Storm's Weekend with Rachael." Journal of the Learning Sciences 9(3): 329-372.

Bryant, S., A. Forte and A. Bruckman (2005). Becoming Wikipedian: Transformation of Participation in a Collaborative Online Encyclopedia. GROUP International Conference on Supporting Group Work, Sanibel Island, FL.

Buckingham, D. (1993). Children talking television: The making of television literacy. London, Falmer.

Buckingham, D. and A. Burn (2007). "Game Literacy in Theory and Practice." Journal of Educational Multimedia and Hypermedia 16(3): 323-349.

Burnham, V. (2001). Supercade: A Visual History of the Videogame Age 1971-1984. Cambridge, Mass, MIT Press.

Byron, S., S. Curran and D. McCarthy (2006). Game On! From Pong to Oblivion. London, Headline Publishing Group.

Byron, T. (2008). "Safer Chlidren in a Digital World: The Report of the Byron Review." Retrieved March 28, 2008, from http://www.dfes. gov.uk/byronreview/.

Caillois, R. (1961). Man, Play and Games. New York, The Free Press.

Castronova, E. (2001). "Virtual Worlds: A First-Hand Account of Market and Society on the Cyberian Frontier." CESifo Working Paper Series No. 618.

Castronova, E. (2006). "On the Research Value of Large Games: Natural Experiments in Norrath and Camelot." Games and Culture 1(2): 163-186.

Chan, C. (1999). Knowledge Building and Belief Change in Computer Supported Collaborative Learning. Meeting of the European Association for Research on Learning and Instruction, Goteburg, Sweden.

Chan, C. K. K. and J. Van Aalst (2003). Student's Self-Reported Beliefs and Attitudes and Knowledge and Learning in Knowledge-Building Classrooms. Annual Meeting of the American Educational Research Association, Chicago, April 21-25.

Chen, K. (2003). "Civilization and its Disk Contents." Radical Society 30(2): 95-107.

Church, D. (1999). Formal Abstract Design Tools. Game Developer.

Collins, A., J. S. Brown and S. E. Newman (1989). Cognitive Apprenticeship: Teaching the Crafts of Reading, Writing, and Mathematics. Knowing, Learning, and Instruction: Essays in Honor of Robert Glaser. L. B. Resnick. Hillsdale, NJ, Lawrence Erlbaum Associates: 453-494.

Commander, N. E. and B. D. Smith (1996). "Learning Logs: A tool for cognitive monitoring." Journal of Adolescent & Adult Literacy 39(6): 446-453.

Connery, R. (1998). "The Unoficcial Quake II FAQ v1.8 Standard Revision." Retrieved December 20, 2007, from http://q2faq.planetquake. gamespy.com/#IV.1.

Consalvo, M. (2007). Cheating: Gaining Advantage in Videogames. Cambridge, MIT Press.

Cope, B. and M. Kalantzis, Eds. (2000). Multiliteracies: Literacy Learning and the design of social futures. London, Routledge.

Cordova, D. and M. R. Lepper (1996). "Intrinsic Motivation and the Process of Learning: Beneficial Effets of Contextualization, Personalization, and Choice." Journal of Educational Psychology 88(4): 715-730.

Costikyan, G. (1994). I have no words & I must design. Interactive Fantasy.

Cragg, A., C. Taylor and B. Toombs. (2006). "BBFC Video Games Report." British Board of Film Classification. from http:// www.bbfc.co.uk/downloads/pub/Policy%20and%20Research/ BBFC%20Video%20Games%20Report.pdf.

Crawford, C. (1984). The Art of Computer Game Design. Berkeley, Osborne/McGraw-Hill.

Crawford, C. (2003). Chris Crawford on Game Design. Indianapolis, Indiana, New Riders Publishing.

Crogan, P. (2004). "The Game Thing: Ludology and Other Theory Games." Media International Australia 2004(110): 10-18.

Crowley, K. and M. Jacobs (2002). Islands of expertise and the development of family scientific literacy. Learning Conversations in Museums. G. Leinhardt, K. Crowley and K. Knutson. Mahwah, NJ, Lawrence Erlbaum.

Culin, S. (1907). Games of the North American Indians. Twenty Fourth Annual Report of the Bureau of American Ethnology, 1902-1903. Washington DC, Government Printing Office: 1-840.

Cummings, M. (2003). Knowledge Building Discourse Offline: A Teacher's Perspective. Annual meeting of the American Educational Research Association, Chicago, USA.

D'Ambrosio, B. S. (1995). "Implementing the Professional Standards for Teaching Mathematics." Mathematics Teacher 88(9): 770-772.

Davis, G. (2002). Game Noir: The Construction of Virtual Subjectivity in Computer Gaming. Honors Thesis in Interdisciplinary Studies in Humanities, Stanford University: 111.

Dipietro, M., R. E. Ferdig, J. Boyer and E. W. Black (2007). "Towards a framework for understanding electronic educational gaming." Journal of Educational Multimedia and Hypermedia 16(3): 225-248.

Donovan, M. S., J. D. Bransford and J. W. E. Pellegrino (1999). How People Learn: Bridging Research and Practice, National Academy Press.

Du, H. S. and C. Wagner (2005). Learning with Weblogs: An Empirical Investigation. Proceedings of the 38th Hawaii International Conference on System Sciences, Hawaii.

Dunnigan, J. F. (1992). The Complete Wargames Handbook Revised Edition. New York, William Morrow and Company.

Eco, U. (1979). "Can television teach?" Screen Education 31: 15-24.

Edelson, D. (1998). Realizing authentic science learning through the adaptation of scientific practice. International Handbook of Science Education. B. J. Fraser and K. G. Tobin. Dordrecht, Kluwer: 317-331.

Edelson, D., D. Gordin and R. D. Pea (1999). "Addressing the Challenges of Inquiry-Based Learning through Technology and Curriculum Design." The Journal of the Learning Sciences 8(3/4): 391-450.

Eisenhardt, K. M. (1989). "Building Theories from Case Study Research." Academy of Management Review 14(4): 532-550.

Elen, J. and G. Clarebout (2001). "An Invasion in the Classroom: Influence of an Ill-Structured Innovation on Instructional and Epistemological Beliefs." Learning Environments Research 4: 87-105.

Ellis, J. and A. Bruckman (2002). What Do Kids Learn from Adults Online? Examining Student-Elder Discourse in Palaver Tree. Proceedings of ICLS 2002, International Conference of the Learning Sciences. Seattle, WA.

Elverdam, C. and E. Aarseth (2007). "Game Classification and Game Design: Construction Through Critical Analysis." Games and Culture 2(1): 3-22.

Emig, J. (1977). "Writing as a mode of learning." College Composition and Communication 28: 122-127.

ESA (2005). "Entertainment Software Association (ESA) - Essential Facts About the Computer and Video Game Industry."

ESA. (2008). "Third Party Views: Recent Editorials and Commentaries Related to the Computer and Video Game Industry." Retrieved Feb 6, 2008, from http://www.theesa.com/facts/third_party_views.php.

Eskelinen, M. (2001). "The Gaming Situation." Game Studies 1(1).

Eskelinen, M. (2004). Towards Computer Game Studies. First Person: New Media as Story, Performance, and Game. N. Wardrip-Fruin and P. Harrigan. Cambridge, Mass, The MIT Press: 36-44.

Fabricatore, C., M. Nussbaum and R. Rosas (2002). "Playability in Action Videogames: A Qualitative Design Model." Human Computer Interaction 17(4): 311-368.

Falstein, N. (2004). "The 400 Project." Retrieved Oct 29, 2004, from http://www.theinspiracy.com/400_project.htm.

Feher, E. and K. Rice (1988). "Shadows and anti-images: Children's conceptions of light and vision II." Science Education 72: 637-649.

Feshbach, S. and R. D. Singer (1971). Television and agression: An experimental field study. San Francisco, CA, Jossey-Bass.

Fleiss, J. L. (1971). "Measuring nomnal scale agreement among many raters." Psychological Bulleting 76: 378-382.

Forte, A. and A. Bruckman (2006). From Wikipedia to the Classroom: Exploring Online Publication and Learning. Proceedings of the 7th International Conference of the Learning Sciences, Bloomington, IN.

Forte, A. and A. Bruckman (2007). Constructing text: Wiki as a toolkit for (collaborative?) learning. Proceedings of the OOPSLA/ACM 2007 International Symposium on Wikis (WikiSym). Montreal, Quebec, Canada: 31-42.

Friedl, M. (2002). Online Game Interactivity Theory. Hingham, MA, Charles River Media.

Fullerton, T. (2005). The Play's the Thing: Practicing Play as Community Foundation and Design Technique. Changing Views: Worlds in Play, DIGRA 2005, Vancouver, Canada.

Gee, J. P. (2003). What Video Games have to Teach us about Learning and Literacy. New York, PalGrave-McMillan.

Gee, J. P. (2005). "Why are videogames good for learning?" Retrieved April 8, 2008, from http://adlcommunity.net/file.php/23/GrooveFiles/John%20Gee%20GAPPS/Gee%20J%20Why%20Are%20Video%20Games%20Good%20.pdf.

Gilster, P. (1997). Digital Literacy. New York, Wiley.

Gingold, C. (2003). Miniature Gardens & Magic Crayons: Games, Spaces, & Worlds. School of Literature, Culture, & Communication. Atlanta, Georgia Institute of Technology: 123.

Glaser, B. and A. Strauss (1967). The Discovery of Grounded Theory: Strategies for Qualitative Research. Chicago, Aldine.

Griffiths, M. D. (1999). "Violent Video Games and Aggression: A Review of the Literature." Aggression and Violent Behavior 4(2): 203-212.

Guesne, E. (1985). Light. Children's ideas in science. R. Driver, E. Guesne and A. Tiberghien. Philadelphia, PA, Open University Press: 11-26.

Guzdial, M., P. Ludovice, M. Realff, T. Morely and K. Carroll (2002). When Collaboration Doesn't Work. International Conference of the Learning Sciences, Seattle, Lawrence Erlbaum Associates.

Hill, C. M., M. Cummings and J. van Aalst (2003). Activity Theory as a Framework for Analyzing Participation within a Knowledge Building Community. Annual meeting of the American Educational Research Association, Chicago, IL.

Hoffman, M. and J. Blake (2003). "Computer Literacy: Today and Tomorrow." Journal of Computing Sciences in Colleges 18(5): 221-233.

Holopainen, J., S. Bjork and J. Kuittinen (2007). Teaching Gameplay Design Patterns. Organizing and Learning through Gaming and Simulation, Proceedings of ISAGA 2007. I. Mayer and H. Mastik. Delft, Eburon.

Hudson, J. and A. Bruckman (2005). Using Empirical Data to Reason About Internet Research Ethics. Proceedings of the 2005 Ninth European Conference on Computer-Supported Collaborative Work. H. Gellersen, K. Schmidt, M. Beaudouin-Lafon and W. Mackay. Dordrecht, The Netherlands, Springer: 287-306.

Huizinga, J. (1954). Homo Ludens. Madrid, Alianza Editorial.

Ito, K. (2005). Possibilities of Non-Commercial Games: The Case of Amateur Role Playing Games Designers in Japan. Changing Views: Worlds in Play, Selected Papers of DIGRA 2005. S. de Castell and J. Jenson. Vancouver, Canada: 135-145.

Jenkins, H. (2003). "Transmedia Storytelling." Technology Review(January).

Jenkins, H. (2006). Convergence Culture: Where Old and New Media Collide. New York, New York University Press.

Jenkins, H. (2007). "Transmedia Storytelling 101." Confessions of an Aca-Fan. Retrieved November 27, 2007, from http://www. henryjenkins.org/2007/03/transmedia_storytelling_101.html.

Jones, S. (2003). "Let the games begin: Gaming technology and entertainment among college students." Pew Internet and American Life Project. Retrieved March 10, 2008, from http://www.pewinternet.org/pdfs/ PIP_College_Gaming_Reporta.pdf.

Joseph, D. and D. C. Nacu (2003). "Designing Interesting Learning Environments When the Medium Isn't Enough." Convergence 9(2): 84-115.

Juul, J. (2001). "The repeatedly lost art of studying games." Game Studies 1(1).

Juul, J. (2003). The Game, the Player, the World: Looking for a Heart of Gameness. Level Up: Digital Games Research Conference Proceedings. M. Copier and J. Raessens. Utrecht, Utrecht University: 30-45.

Juul, J. (2005). Half-Real. Cambridge, Mass, The MIT Press.

Kafai, Y. (1995). Minds in play: Computer game design as a context for children's learning. New Jersey, Lawrence Erlbaum Associates.

Kafai, Y. (1996). Learning Design by Making Games. Constructionism in Practice. Y. Kafai and M. Resnick. Mahwah, New Jersey, Lawrence Erlbaum Associates.

Ketelhut, D. J., C. Dede, J. Clarke, B. Nelson and C. Bowman (In Press). Studying situated learning in a multi-user virtual environment. Assessment of problem solving using simulations. E. Baker, J. Dickieson, W. Wulfeck and H. O'Neil. Mahwah, NJ, Lawrence Erlbaum Associates.

Kirsch, I. S., A. Jungeblut, L. Jenkins and A. Kolstad (2002). Adult Literacy in America: A First Look at the Findings of the National Adult Literacy Survey, 3rd Edition, National Center for Education Statistics - U.S. Department of Education.

Klostermann, C. (2006, June 30, 2006). "The Lester Bangs of Videogames." Esquire. from http://www.esquire.com/features/ ESQ0706KLOSTER_66.

Kobrin, D., E. Abbott, J. Elinwood and D. Horton (1993). "Learning history by doing history." Educational Leadership 50(7): 39-41.

Kolodner, J. L., P. J. Camp, D. Crismond, B. Fasse, J. Gray, J. Holbrook, S. Puntambekar and M. Ryan (2003). "Problem-Based Learning Meets Case-Based Reasoning in the Middle-School Science Classroom: Putting Learning by Design Into Practice." The Journal of the Learning Sciences 12(4): 495-547.

Kolodner, J. L., D. Crismond, J. Gray, J. Holbrook and S. Puntambekar (1998). Learning by Design from Theory to Practice. International Conference of the Learning Sciences, Atlanta, GA.

Kolodner, J. L. and M. Guzdial (2000). Theory and Practice of Case-Based Learning Aids. Theoretical Foundations of Learning Environments. D. Jonassen and S. Land. Mahwah, NJ, Lawrence Erlbaum Associates.

Koster, R. (2004). A Theory of Fun for Game Design, Paraglyph.

Kreimeier, B. (2002). "The Case for Game Design Patterns." Gamasutra. Retrieved Oct 29, 2004, from http://www.gamasutra.com/ features/20020313/kreimeier_01.htm.

Kücklich, J. (2007). Rez: Merging Sound and Space. Space Time Play. F. von Borries, S. Walz and M. Bottger. Basel, Switzerland, Birkhauser.

Laurel, B. (1991). Computers as Theatre. Reading, Massachusetts, Addison-Wesley Publishing.

Lave, J. and E. Wenger (1991). Situated Learning: Legitimate Peripheral Participation. Cambridge, UK, Cambridge University Press.

Leuf, B. and W. Cunningham (2001). The Wiki Way: Quick Collaboration on the Web, Addison-Wesley.

Linn, M. C., P. Bell and S. Hsi (1998). "Using the Internet to Enhace Student Understanding of Science: The Knowledge Integration Environment." Interactive Learning Environments 6(1-2): 4-38.

Lombard, M., J. Snyder-Duch and C. Companella (2002). "Content Analysis in Mass Communication: Assessment and Reporting of Intercoder Reliability." Human Communication Research 28(4): 587-604.

Lundgren, S. and S. Björk (2003). Describing Computer-Augmented Games in Terms of Interaction. Technologies for Interactive Digital Storytelling and Entertainment (TIDSE), Darmstadt, Germany.

Malone, T. W. (1980). What makes things fun to learn? A Study of instrinsically motivating computer games. Department of Psychology. Stanford, Stanford University.

Malone, T. W. (1981). "Toward a theory of intrinsically motivating instruction." Cognitive Science 4: 333-369.

Mateas, M. (2002). Interactive Drama, Art, and Artificial Intelligence. School of Computer Science. Pittsburgh, Carnegie Mellon University.

Mateas, M. (2003). Expressive AI: Games and Artificial Intelligence. Level Up: Digital Games Research Conference, Utrecht, Netherlands.

Mateas, M. and A. Stern (2004). Natural Language Processing In Facade: Surface-text Processing. Technologies for Interactive Digital Storytelling and Entertainment (TIDSE), Darmstadt, Germany, June 2004.

Mäyrä, F. (2005). "The Quiet Revolution: Three Theses for the Future of Game Studies." DiGRA Retrieved Jan 26, 2006, 2006, from http://digra.org/hardcore/hc4.

Moore, D. and F. Dwyer (1994). Visual Literacy: A spectrum of visual learning. Englewood Cliffs, NJ, Educational Technology Publications.

Murray, J. H. (1997). Hamlet on the Holodeck: The Future of Narrative in Cyberspace. New York, The Free Press.

Murray, J. H. (2005). The Last Word on Ludology v Narratology in Game Studies. International DiGRA Conference 2005, Vancouver, Canada.

Nardi, B. A., D. J. Schiano, M. Gumbrecht and L. Swartz (2004). "Why we Blog." Communications of the ACM 47(12): 41-46.

Navarro, A. (2007). "Rayman Raving Rabids Review (GBA)." Gamespot. Retrieved Jan 10, 2007, from http://www.gamespot.com/gba/action/rayman4/review.html?sid=6164240&print=1.

Neuendorf, K. A. (2002). The content analysis guidebook. Thousand Oaks, CA, Sage.

Neuman, W. L. (2000). Social Research Methods (4th Edition). Boston, MA, Allyn & Bacon.

O'Neill, D. K. and L. M. Gomez (1998). Sustaining mentoring relationships on-line. Proceedings of the 1998 ACM conference on Computer supported cooperative work: 325-334.

Pagulayan, R. J., K. Keeker, D. Wixon, R. Romero and T. Fuller (2003). User-centered design in games. Handbook for Human-Computer Interaction in Interactive Systems. J. Jacko and S. Sears. Mahwah, NJ, Lawrence Erlbaum Associates: 883-906.

Papert, S. (1980). Mindstorms : children, computers, and powerful ideas. New York, Basic Books.

Papert, S. (1991). Situating Constructionism. Constructionism. I. P. Harel, Seymour. Norwood, NJ, Ablex Publishing Company: 1-11.

Parlett, D. (1999). The Oxford History of Board Games. Oxford and New York, Oxford University Press.

Parr, C. S., T. Jones and N. Butler Songer (2002). CyberTracker in BioKIDS: Customization of a PDA-Based Scientific Data Collection Application for Inquiry Learning. Keeping Learning Complex: The Proceedings of the Fifth International Conference of Learning Sciences. P. Bell, R. Stevens and T. Satwicz: 574-575.

Perlis, A. J. (1962). The Computer in the University. Computers and the World of the Future. M. Greenberger. Cambridge, Massachusetts, The MIT Press.

Perry, T. E. and P. Wallich (1983). "Design case history: the Atari Video Computer System." IEEE Spectrum(March): 45-51.

Piaget, J. (1962). Play, dreams and imitation in childhood. New York, Norton.

Piaget, J. (1972). The Principles of Genetic Epistemology. New York, Basic Books.

Pratchett, R. (2005). Gamers in the UK: Digital play, digital lifestyles, BBC Creative Research and Development: 1-25.

Reagin, J. (2004). Theoretical and Practical Applications of Emergent Technology in ELT Classrooms; How the 'Blog' Can Change English Language Teaching. The Fourth International Symposium on ELT in China, Beiking, PRC.

Resnick, M., A. Bruckman and F. Martin (1996). "Pianos Not Stereos: Creating Computational Construction Kits." Interactions 3(5): 41-50.

Rogoff, B. (1994). "Developing Understanding of the Idea of Communities of Learners." Mind, Culture, and Activity 1(4): 209-229.

Rollings, A. and D. Morris (2000). Game Architecture and Design. Scottsdale, Arizona, Coriolis.

Roth, W. M. (1998). Designing Communities. Dordrecht, Kluwer Academic Publishers.

Rouse III, R. (2001). Game Design: Theory & Practice. Plano, TX, Wordware Publishing Inc.

Salen, K. (2007). "Gaming Literacies: A Game Design Study in Action." Journal of Educational Multimedia and Hypermedia 16(3): 301-322.

Salen, K. and E. Zimmerman (2004). Rules of Play: Game Design Fundamentals. Cambridge, Massachusetts, The MIT Press.

Scardamalia, M. and C. Bereiter (1991). "Higher Levels of Agency for Children in Knowledge Building: A Challenge for the Design of New Knowledge Media." The Journal of the Learning Sciences 1(1): 37-68.

Scardamalia, M. and C. Bereiter (1994). "Computer Support for Knowledge-Building Communities." The Journal of the Learning Sciences 3(3): 265-283.

Scardamalia, M. and C. Bereiter (2002). Knowledge Building. Encyclopedia of Education, 2nd Edition. New York, Macmillan Reference.

Schank, R., T. R. Berman and K. A. Macpherson (1999). Learning by Doing. Instructional-Design Theories and Models. C. M. Reigeluth. Mahwah, New Jersey, Lawrence Erlbaum Associates.

Schell, J. and J. Shochet (2001). Designing Interactive Theme Park Rides: Lessons Learned from Creating Disney's Pirates of the Caribbean-Battle for the Buccaneer Gold. Game Developers Conference, San Jose, CA, March 20-24.

Schon, D. (1987). Educating the Reflective Practitioner: Toward a New Design for Teaching and Learning in the Professions. San Francisco, CA, Jossey-Bass Inc.

Seipp, C. (2002). "Online uprising." American Journalism Review 24(5): 42-48.

Sellers, J. (2001). Arcade Fever: The Fan's Guide to the Golden Age of Videogames. London, Running Press.

Sfard, A. (1998). "On two metaphors for learning and the dangers of choosing just one." Educational Researcher 27: 4-13.

Shaffer, D. W. (2006). How Computer Games Help Children Learn. New York, Palgrave Macmillan.

Shaffer, D. W. and M. Resnick (1999). ""Thick" Authenticity: New Media and Authentic Learning." Journal of Interactive Learning Research 10(2): 195-215.

Shapiro, B. (1994). What children bring to light: A constructivist perspective on children's learning in science. New York, Teacher's College.

Sherry, J. L. (2001). "The Effects of Violent Video Games on Aggression." Human Communication Research 27(3): 409-431.

Songer, N. (1996). "Exploring Learning Opportunities in Coordinated Network-Enhanced Classrooms: A Case of Kids as Global Scientists." The Journal of the Learning Sciences 5(4): 297-327.

Spencer, M. (1986). "Emergent Literacies: A site for analysis." Language Arts 63(5): 442-53.

Squire, K. D. (2005). "Changing the game: What happens when videogames enter the classroom?" Innovate 6(1).

Stahl, G. (2001). "Webguide: Guiding Collaborative Learning on the Web with Perspectives." Journal of Interactive Media In Education 1.

Stang, B., H. C. Bjorne, M. Østerholt and E. Hoftun (2006). The Book of Games Volume 1. Ottawa ON, Canada, gameXplore

Steinkuehler, C. (2006). "Massively Multiplayer Online Video Gaming as Participation in a Discourse." Mind, Culture, and Activity 13(1): 38-52.

Stiler, G. M. and T. Philleo (2003). "Blogging and Blogspots: An Alternative Format for Encouraging Reflective Practice Among Preservice Teachers." Education 123: 789-797.

Stuart, K. (2005). "State of play: is there a role for the New Games Journalism." Retrieved Feb 26, 2008, from http://blogs.guardian.co.uk/games/archives/game_culture/2005/02/state_of_play_is_there_a_role_for_the_new_games_journalism.html.

Sykes, J. and S. Brown (2003). Affective Gaming: Measuring Emotion Through the Gamepad. CHI '03 Extended Abstracts on Human Factors in Computing Systems, ACM Press: 732-733.

Taylor, T. L. (2006). Play Between Worlds. Cambridge, MIT Press.

Turkle, S. (1995). Life on the screen : identity in the age of the Internet. New York, Simon & Schuster.

van Aalst, J. and C. K. K. Chan (2007). "Student-Directed Assessment of Knowledge Building Using Electronic Portfolios." Journal of the Learning Sciences 16(2): 175-220.

Viegas, F., M. Wattenberg and D. Kushal (2004). Studying Cooperation and Conflict between Authors with history flow Visualizations. CHI 2004, Vienna, Austria.

Vygotsky, L. S. (1978). Mind in Society: The Development of Higher Psychological Processes. Cambridge, Massachusetts, Harvard University Press.

Wenger, E. (1998). Communities of Practice. Cambridge, Cambridge University Press.

Williams, D. (2005). "Bridging the methodological divide in game research." Simulation & Gaming 36(4): 447-463.

Wiltse, E. M. (2004). Blog, Blog, Blog: Experiences with web logs in journalism classes. International Symposium on Online Journalism.

Wittgenstein, L. (1963). Philosophical Investigations. New York, The Macmillan Company.

Zagal, J. P. and A. Bruckman (2005). "From Samba Schools to Computer Clubhouses: Cultural Institutions as Learning Environments." Convergence 11(1): 88-105.

Zagal, J. P. and A. Bruckman (2007). GameLog: Fostering Reflective Gameplaying for Learning. 2007 ACM SIGGRAPH Symposium on Videogames, San Diego, CA, ACM Press.

Zagal, J. P., M. Mateas, C. Fernandez-Vara, B. Hochhalter and N. Lichti (2005). Towards an Ontological Language for Game Analysis. Changing Views: Worlds in Play, Selected Papers of DIGRA 2005. S. de Castell and J. Jenson. Vancouver, Canada: 3-14.

Zagal, J. P., M. Mateas, C. Fernandez-Vara, B. Hochhalter and N. Lichti (2007). Towards an Ontological Language for Game Analysis. Worlds in Play: International Perspectives on Digital Games Research. S. de Castell and J. Jenson. New York, Peter Lang: 21-35.

Zagal, J. P., J. Rick and I. Hsi (2006). "Collaborative Games: Lessons learned from board games." Simulation and Gaming 37(1): 24-40.

VITA

JOSÉ P. ZAGAL

Dr. José P. Zagal is a game designer, scholar, and researcher. He is Assistant Professor at the College of Computing and Digital Media at DePaul University where he teaches game design and ethics. His research work explores the development of frameworks for describing, analyzing, and understanding games from a critical perspective to help inform the design of better games. He is also interested in supporting games literacy through the use of collaborative learning environments. Dr. Zagal is on the editorial board of the International Journal of Gaming and Computer-Mediated Simulations and the Journal of the Canadian Gaming Studies Organization. He is also a member of the executive board of the Digital Games Research Association (DiGRA). José received his PhD in computer science from Georgia Institute of Technology in 2008, his M.Sc. in engineering sciences and a B.S. in industrial engineering from Pontificia Universidad Católica de Chile in 1999 and 1997.